Discerning the Spirits

Calvin Institute of Christian Worship Liturgical Studies Series

The Calvin Institute of Christian Worship Liturgical Studies Series, edited by John D. Witvliet, is designed to promote reflection on the history, theology, and practice of Christian worship and to stimulate worship renewal in Christian congregations. Contributions include writings by pastoral worship leaders from a wide range of communities and scholars from a wide range of disciplines. The ultimate goal of these contributions is to nurture worship practices that are spiritually vital and theologically rooted.

Published Volumes

GATHER INTO ONE
Praying and Singing Globally
C. Michael Hawn

THE SUBSTANCE OF THINGS SEEN
Art, Faith, and the Christian Community
Robin M. Jensen

WONDERFUL WORDS OF LIFE
*Hymns in American Protestant
History and Theology*
Richard J. Mouw and Mark A. Noll,
Editors

DISCERNING THE SPIRITS
*A Guide to Thinking about
Christian Worship Today*
Cornelius Plantinga Jr. and
Sue A. Rozeboom

VOICING GOD'S PSALMS
Calvin Seerveld

MY ONLY COMFORT
*Death, Deliverance, and Discipleship
in the Music of Bach*
Calvin R. Stapert

A MORE PROFOUND ALLELUIA
Theology and Worship in Harmony
Leanne Van Dyk, Editor

CHRISTIAN WORSHIP IN REFORMED
CHURCHES PAST AND PRESENT
Lukas Vischer, Editor

Discerning the Spirits

*A Guide to Thinking about
Christian Worship Today*

Cornelius Plantinga Jr.
Sue A. Rozeboom

WILLIAM B. EERDMANS PUBLISHING COMPANY
GRAND RAPIDS, MICHIGAN / CAMBRIDGE, U.K.

© 2003 Wm. B. Eerdmans Publishing Co.
All rights reserved

WM. B. EERDMANS PUBLISHING CO.
2140 Oak Industrial Drive N.E., Grand Rapids, Michigan 49505 /
P.O. Box 163, Cambridge CB3 9PU U.K.
www.eerdmans.com

Printed in the United States of America

11   10   09   7   6   5

Library of Congress Cataloging-in-Publication Data

Discerning the spirits: a guide to thinking about Christian worship today /
    Cornelius Plantinga, Jr., Sue A. Rozeboom.
        p.   cm. — (Calvin Institute of Christian Worship liturgical studies series)
    Includes bibliographical references.
    ISBN 978-0-8028-3999-2 (pbk.: alk. paper)
    1. Public worship — United States — Congresses.
    I. Plantinga, Cornelius, 1946-   II. Rozeboom, Sue A.   III. Series.
BV15.D57   2003
264 — dc22

                                                    2003049467

This book has been composed in Cartier Book and Formata
Design by Kevin van der Leek Design Inc.

Contents

Articles

Preface

IT IS PARTICULARLY GRATIFYING to introduce this volume because it is the product of the first collaborative research team sponsored by the Calvin Institute of Christian Worship. The mission of the Worship Institute is "to promote scholarly study of the theology, history, and practice of Christian worship and the renewal of worship in local congregations." We aim to have these twin purposes meld together so that our scholarship contributes to congregational renewal and the renewal we seek and pray for is grounded in thoughtful reflection.

An interdisciplinary research center at a Christian college or seminary is certainly not the only place or even the best place from which to work toward worship renewal. Worship renewal is the common work of a large array of exemplary congregations, thoughtful pastoral leaders and mentors, denominational offices, parachurch organizations, publishers, journals, and professional organizations for preachers, church musicians, and artists. The Holy Spirit works through a vibrant diversity of people and institutions to encourage, challenge, and sustain the life of the church.

The particular virtue of working in the context of a liberal arts college or seminary is the opportunity to see a large landscape, to consider present issues from the multiple perspectives of the whole sweep of Christian history, the worldwide practices of hundreds of ethnic groups, and the entire spectrum of Christian traditions and denominations. Viewing the world through these wide-angled lenses helps us understand particular issues and opportunities more clearly. We come to understand which battles are worth fighting, which issues are truly significant, and which opportunities for collaboration and ministry are most promising.

Colleges are also places for setting aside time for genuine conversations, without the immediate pressure of creating another product to market. In the church, as in contemporary culture, we often are so busy doing or talking that we fail to take time for listening. We often begin conversations by naming what we have to teach or which agenda we are eager to promote rather than asking what we might be able to learn. All of us on the study team that produced this volume would agree that our work together challenged us to listen more attentively.

Collaborative research is particularly energizing work at a Christian college that has genuine interest in the health and vitality of Christian churches. At their best, Christian institutions of higher education promote taking a broad view of culture in time and space and creating spaces for genuine interdisciplinary learning, just like any university. But these efforts are not designed to promote scholarship for its own sake. Rather, the goal is to promote fruitful Christian practice in all facets of society, including the church. Our prayer is that the seeds planted by this volume will bear rich fruit in the life of Christian congregations. We are grateful to President Gaylen Byker and the Board of Trustees of Calvin College for their commitment to serving the church and for their support of our work.

Often, academic research is detailed and analytic, offering comprehensive treatments of primary sources and extensive explications of particular theories or hypotheses. Basic research, whether in science, history, or theology, is necessary both for honing analytical skills and for honest and accurate assessments of particular subjects. Several of the participants in this study group are active and prolific writers in this more technical, academic approach. Yet often this kind of writing speaks to a limited audience, and focuses on a comparatively narrow topic. In contrast, this volume attempts to fill a different genre, synthesizing the data and accumulated wisdom of extensive work in the history, theology, and sociological analysis of contemporary church culture. Our challenge was to address a complex phenomenon ("contemporary" worship), identify which themes, topics, and issues were most important to address, and imagine how they could be discussed in ways that were both accurate and helpful—all in fewer than 200 pages. We are grateful not only to the entire study team for their creative spirit, but especially to Neal Plantinga and Sue Rozeboom, who labored over multiple drafts of outlines and manuscripts in the process of developing this book.

Finally, we are grateful to Lilly Endowment and its Vice President for Religion, Craig Dykstra, for the financial resources to convene the study team that conceived this volume, their commitment to enhance and deepen the life of Christian congregations, and their thoughtful encouragement of our ongoing work.

John D. Witvliet

CALVIN INSTITUTE OF CHRISTIAN WORSHIP

Calvin College and Calvin Theological Seminary

Grand Rapids, Michigan

Introduction

ACCORDING TO SCRIPTURE, wisdom is, broadly speaking, knowledge of God's world and the knack of fitting oneself into it. The wise person knows creation. She knows its boundaries and limits, understands its laws and dynamics, discerns its times and seasons, respects its great dynamics. She knows some of the deep grains and textures of the world because she knows some of the ways of its maker.

Wisdom is a reality-based phenomenon. To be wise is to know reality, to *discern* it. A discerning person notices things, attends to things, picks up on things. She notices the difference between tolerance and forgiveness, for example, and between sentimentality and compassion. In this way, discernment is a mark of wisdom: it shows a kind of attentive respect for reality. The discerning person notices the differences between things, but also the connections between them.[1] She knows creation — what God has put together and what God has kept asunder — and can therefore spot the fractures and alloys introduced by human violation of it. She knows, for instance, the way a particular sort of request can contaminate a friendship. The discerning person, moreover, possesses an eye for the details and

1. See Lewis B. Smedes, *A Pretty Good Person* (San Francisco: Harper and Row, 1990), p. 123.

oddities of reality — the anxieties, for example, that sometimes lie behind ill-bred chitchat, name-dropping, and the overuse of foreign phrases at dinner parties. She knows that kindness sometimes co-exists with stupidity and integrity with humorlessness. She knows that people full of shadows may also be full of a light that causes them. In such and other respects, Lewis Smedes remarks, "a discerning person has the makings of a connoisseur."[2]

But such "cognitive discernment," as Smedes calls it, isn't enough. The really discerning person, the one whose discernment marks genuine wisdom, does not merely inspect reality or analyze it. The one who discerns also loves. The deeply discerning person brings empathy and care to what she knows. Discernment of the hopes and fears of other persons, for example, depends on compassion for them: knowledge of these persons comes in to us only if our hearts go out to them. Only so, Smedes remarks, could Steinbeck have written as he did of Ma Joad or of Rose of Sharon in *The Grapes of Wrath*. Only so can we see behind the status of divorce, or homosexuality, or disability to discover complex persons who possess gifts and wholenesses that are greater than their troubles and unseen by the unloving.

Beyond argument, one way to gain wisdom is to pray. The apostle James wrote to the twelve tribes of the Dispersion (from which our own churches descend), "If any of you is lacking in wisdom, ask God, . . . and it will be given you." James knew — likely from personal experience and certainly from the testimony of Scripture — that

O God, Creator of all that is,
  From the treasures of Your wisdom,
    You have arrayed the universe with
    marvelous order,
      and now govern with skill and might.

You are the true fount of light and wisdom.

Pour forth a ray of Your brightness
  into the darkened places of our minds;
Disperse from our souls
    the twofold darkness
      into which we were born:
  sin and ignorance. . . .

Through Jesus Christ our Lord,
  Amen.

Adapted from a prayer of St. Thomas Aquinas, in *Devoutly I Adore Thee: The Prayers and Hymns of St. Thomas Aquinas* (Manchester, N.H.: Sophia Institute, 1993), p. 41

---

2. Smedes, *Pretty Good Person*, p. 124.

God is "generous" and that he gives "ungrudgingly" (1:5). God freely offers wisdom, but he does want us to ask for it.

Such asking is not often answered by a supernatural inscription on a wall, or a paranormal nudge, or a whisper on the wind. These means are reserved: only a few receive them by special dispensation. In the usual scheme of life, wisdom requires effort. Why else would the inspired pundit of Proverbs urge us "to seek it like silver, and search for it as for hidden treasures" (2:4)? Even James says we must ask, and adds that we must do so with great confidence. A doubter, says James, is "double-minded" and "unstable" and "must not expect to receive anything from the Lord" (1:8).

Wisdom isn't merely *within.* It is often *without.* It is an object, an objective, to be sought and then treasured when attained. It is *without,* which is why our understanding is so often jogged by an article written on a related topic, by a companion's pointed question, or by the "click" and "clack" of *Car Talk:* "Live Larger. Drive Smaller! Not everyone needs an SUV."[3]

Our perceptions are so often sharpened when we discuss an issue with people who are passionate about its outcome, who have studied its subtleties and respect someone else's take on them, too. We contract wisdom not in a vacuum, but in a context, which so often is a dialogue, a conference, a meeting of minds that are open and aware.

Knowing this is so and being himself duly enthused about the topic of worship, John Witvliet, Director of Calvin College's Institute for Christian Worship, secured a grant from the Lilly Endowment. Given generous resources, he gathered a team of Christian men and women to respond to the current state of worship, particularly as it exists in North America. Comprising church musicians, authors, editors, ministers, worship leaders, and educators from eight church traditions and from most of the spectrum of opinion about present-

3. Tom Magliozzi and Ray Magliozzi, *Car Talk,* a joint production of Public Interactive, Inc., and Dewey, Cheetham and Howe. Contents © Dewey, Cheetham and Howe, http://cartalk.cars.com (15 August 2002).

day worship practices, the team met under John's leadership three times for three to five days at a time. On these occasions we team members raised and debated issues about worship today, including the phenomenon of "Contemporary Worship." Discussion topics ranged widely, from inculturation to intergenerational tensions, from the theology of worship to the meaning and role of "taste."

We absorbed each other's insights and challenged each other's judgments. We prayed and worshiped together. We visited churches and attended a conference concurrent with our January meeting (the annual Symposium on Worship and the Arts at Calvin College). We wrote reflective papers, and argued about their finer points. *Discerning the Spirits* is the fruit of our work.

The main structure and argument of this book was conceived and revised in team discussions. After our meetings were completed, we authors distilled the discussions, working papers, e-mails, and ongoing conference calls to generate the main manuscript, presenting the team's work in a single voice, trying to capture the wisdom of our group's discussion in a genre other than a committee report.

The voices of the team members sound throughout the main text of this book, though we authors do not always stop to cite them. Hence the articles included in each chapter: almost all of the team participants present at least one reflection piece that conveys their unique expertise and insight. These reflections, along with quotations from other resources, make this book not merely an essay but a conversation. We hope you are drawn in.

Our aim in this book is not only to discuss worship in North America today but also — and more importantly — to present the fruit of our thinking about the right *tone* for such discussion. Worship is worth arguing about, not least because it is an important aspect of our relationship with God, and because it lies at the crossing between the church and the world, or "Christ and culture." But early in our deliberations we took note of a wonderful distinction in the autobiography of G. K. Chesterton, in which Chesterton says that he and his younger brother Cecil argued for decades, but never quarreled. In fact, writes Chesterton, "both my brother and I would have thought that what's wrong with a quarrel is that it stops a good argument."

It also stops good fellowship. As a team, we came both to believe and to experience the fact that while we Christians have quarreled over worship, and perhaps especially over Contemporary Worship, we needn't. And we shouldn't. Without sentimentality or spinelessness, we should learn from each other, care about each other, and, so far as it lies with us, live in peace together as brothers and sisters in Jesus Christ. To get this far, we do need to practice some of those good manners that lie next door to good morals — listening before we speak, putting the best face on other people's motives, expressing our concerns with minimum necessary force. We need to think not only of what kind of worship we will practice but, before and after that, of what kind of people we will be. Will we be disputants, or conversation partners? Will we try to learn, or only to win? Will we seek to understand each other affectively as well as intellectually, and offer each other a good line of moral and spiritual credit? To put the question in New Testament terms, will we adorn ourselves with those wonderful garments — humility, kindness, patience, forbearance — that fit people who have been "raised with Christ"?

Discerning the Spirits is a team's witness to the importance of telling the truth in love, and, we hope, an example of doing it. For the chance to try, we want to thank the Lilly Endowment, the Calvin College Institute for Christian Worship, David Vroege, who transcribed our first two proceedings, and John Witvliet, who conceived and directed this project with his exemplary blend of intelligence and grace.

C.P. Jr.

S.A.R.

Chapter 1

The Things of the Spirit

THE TROUBLE WITH LOVING the things of the Spirit, as Robert C. Roberts once wrote, is that "the Holy Spirit isn't the only spirit around." The Holy Spirit is in competition with a lot of other spirits, and some of them look as if *they* come from God too. They look as if they might be life-giving spirits. They feel as if they might be comforting spirits. The spirit of personal ambition, for example, can look like holy zeal. The spirit of aesthetic pleasure can feel like adoration of God. The spirit of envy can sound like the hunger for social justice. What's more, these spirits show up not only on TV but also in church, where they compete with God for our loyalty. When we embrace them instead of God we commit idolatry, but perhaps unconsciously, given their omnipresence. In any case, what we clearly need is a particular gift of the Holy Spirit, namely, the ability to *discern* spirits — to identify them, to tell them apart, and to disentangle them from the Spirit of God.[1]

At no time do we need this ability more urgently than when we think about the changes that have come upon Christian worship in North America within the last twenty-five years, and especially the

---

1. Robert C. Roberts, *The Strengths of a Christian* (Philadelphia: Westminster, 1984), p. 19.

The Ridiculous Incongruity of Worship

Justo L. González

On the nature of Christian worship, perhaps we ought to begin by stating that the acceptance of worship is always an act of God's grace. There is no worship, no music, no prayer, no sermon, in itself so good that God has to accept it. Just as we are sinners whose life God redeems by grace, we are all mumbling stutterers whose words and music God accepts by grace. Just as we cannot attain heaven by a ladder of good works, so can we not attain God's ear by a scale of beautiful notes.

By its very nature worship, no matter how aesthetically pleasing, is ridiculously incongruous. To think that we can really offer praise so worthy that God would accept it on its own merit is the height of folly. This judgment of ridiculous incongruity must be equally applied to all worship, from the most elemental to the most sophisticated. We cannot overcome it with the well-modulated motifs of a Bach fugue, and we cannot overcome it with the most sincerely felt and most exuberantly expressed joy of contemporary "praise" songs.

This is true not only of the style of worship but also of its content. What this means is that theology *(for worship ought to be theologically sound)* must be very clear that its task is not to make worship acceptable to God. Just as Christian ethics does not seek to make our actions acceptable to God, so theology should not seek to make our worship acceptable to God. That is best left up to God's grace. In worship we not only celebrate God's graceful acceptance of ourselves; we also offer unacceptable gifts, trusting that the same grace that has accepted us will accept them.

---

package of changes often called "Contemporary Worship" (a term we capitalize to distinguish it from present-day worship, only some of which would be classified as "Contemporary"). Here is a movement that some praise as revival and others condemn as apostasy. From San Diego, California, to Bangor, Maine, the movement has renewed some congregations and troubled or even split others. In fact, it has changed the way lots of Christians identify themselves — no longer first as "Methodist" or "Presbyterian," no longer first as "liberal" or "evangelical" or "fundamental." Nowadays, just as some generations of Americans identify themselves according to the kind of music they listen to, so a number of Christians think of themselves primarily in terms of their style of worship. They attend "Contemporary Worship" or else "traditional worship," and they may make their choice with a good deal of passion. Or they may elect one of the forms of "blended worship" that combine classic hymns, contemporary Christian ballads, and popular gospel choruses, and feel that this choice, too, represents the compromise or settlement of a spirited debate.

To its advocates, Contemporary Worship represents the fresh breeze of the Spirit of God blowing through the church. These Christians have chafed at worship that seems to them stale. Organ preludes, sedate preachments, contrived silences, formulaic responses, peculiar hymn texts — these and other features of so-called traditional worship have left them feeling "sore oppressed," to quote one of the hymns they would like to escape. They wonder, How did the worship of God get to be so *boring?* Why shouldn't we worship in the ways that we actually talk and sing? Why shouldn't we worship in a way that has a chance of connecting with seekers — including the seekers within our own families?

When given the opportunity to worship God in their popular idiom, the advocates of Contemporary Worship think as our ancestors did when they were handed a Bible translated into their own language: "At last! At last we are liberated to encounter God in our natural voice!"

> "[W]orship is going on all the time in heaven, and when we worship we are joining that which is already happening. . . ."
>
> John Wimber, "Worship: Intimacy with God," http://www.vineyardboise.org/specialized_ministries/ worship/wimber_worship.htm (1 August 2003)

But to more classically minded Christians, Contemporary Worship represents the blowing not of the Spirit of God but of the spirit of the age. When they attend their church's worship on Sunday morning and discover that their minister now acts like an emcee, or that the sanctuary has been darkened in order to spotlight a "Christian performing artist," these Christians believe that their church has sold its soul. Worship seems less like the company of saints and martyrs than like a nightclub that forgot to close. So they wonder, Why outfit the gospel in an ethos that clashes with it? Why stand for worldly entertainment, rather than against it? Why can't believers worship God without trying simultaneously to amuse a TV-sated audience?

When given a chance to worship in a so-called "traditional" idiom, the opponents of Contemporary Worship think as our forebears did when they were handed a Bible translated into their own language: "At last! At last we have the prophets and apostles, who liberate us to encounter God aside from the tyranny of contemporary fashion!"

Present-day worship practices have stimulated a good deal of argument among Christians, and rightly so. On the whole, worship *deserves* a good argument, since (as we noted in the introduction) worship stands right at the intersection of the church and the world, or of "Christ and culture." In worship, as in all else, Christians want to know how to celebrate the gospel in such a way as to show its attraction, but also in such a way that it's still the gospel that gets celebrated, and not some cheaper grace of our own. And so we argue, and, regrettably, sometimes even quarrel: Can the gospel be conveyed today with habits and tunes that are more than three hundred years old, or only with JumboTron screens and PowerPoint presentations?

"[W]e worship in the Spirit, and as we do so we are taking our place amongst the angels and archangels and all the company of heaven. . . . Heaven is not a long way away."

N. T. Wright, "Freedom and Framework, Spirit and Truth: Rediscovering Biblical Worship," *The January Series,* Calvin College (11 January 2002)

This intersection between "the church and the world" or "Christ and culture" is one where Christians have debated before, and the debate has never ceased. It has simply been passed down, one generation to the next, for as long as the Christian church has existed. Whenever Christians have sought to preach, teach, worship, or witness in forms adapted from their immediate, local culture, their brothers and sisters in Christ have wondered whether the church should be more circumspect. To ally with culture to serve the purposes of grace is to take the risk of corrupting the gospel — which (as we shall explore later) is something like the risk of the incarnation itself.

In any case, disagreements arise, often sharp ones.

We should take note that many contemporary disputes, such as those on university campuses, flare among people whose contrary loyalties give them scant hope of resolving their dispute, or even of setting its tone. The reason is that the disputants are skeptical of the human quest for truth and of the role of honest argument in support of this quest. Moreover, apart from their common skepticism, they may also be committed to opposing philosophies of life, or, as it is often put these days, to "different core values." In fact, given their joint skepticism and root opposition, both parties may acknowledge up front that agreement is beyond their reach, that serious debate is a doubtful or even pointless exercise, and that the only plausible outcome of a tussle between them is that one will out-shout or out-maneuver the other.

Here Christians enjoy some of the glorious liberty of the children of God: they may hope for serious discussion leading toward convergence, and perhaps even a degree of consensus. After all, given their doctrines of God and creation, Christians think there is such a thing as reality, "the way things are," and such a thing as truth, a reliable account of reality. Christians also think that by disciplined study of God's revelation we can gain wisdom, especially if we help correct each other's prejudices and self-deceptions with serious discussion.

> *"Eternal, incomprehensible, and invisible God, infinite in power, wisdom and goodness; dwelling in the light which no man can approach, where thousand thousands minister unto thee, and ten thousand times ten thousand stand before thee. . . . We come to thee at thy call and worship at thy footstool."*
>
> Richard Baxter, The Savoy Liturgy 1661, in *Liturgies of the Western Church* (Philadelphia: Fortress Press, 1980), p. 385

Part of the truth that Christians jointly confess is a whole cluster of powerfully unifying realities. We believe in one God: the Father, the Son, and the Holy Spirit. We have "one Lord, one faith, one baptism" (Eph. 4:5). We confess one holy catholic church, across the world and across time, and we are conscious of worshiping in the company of its saints and martyrs. We tell the same story of redemption and jointly hope for its everlasting denouement. Moreover, Christians share a general view of the world and of our calling in it, namely, that the world has been created and redeemed by God, through Jesus Christ, and that those in union with Christ should "live for the praise of his glory" by "seeking first the kingdom of God" (Eph. 1:12; cf. Matt. 6:33).

How might this vocation be pursued?

Even at a general level, Christians answer this question in several ways, but one venerable answer is that in response to God's grace we ought to lead lives distinguished by certain features of godliness or piety. We ought to make good works our "way of life" (Eph. 2:10) and good attitudes our "central business," as Jonathan Edwards put it. On this view a Christian's vocation largely consists in acquiring those "religious affections" or "holy practices" that fit people who belong to Jesus Christ.

To sketch such a life and its practices, the New Testament offers sections of "parenesis," or instructions for godly living.[2] These are glad invitations and exhortations for people who would follow Jesus. "Let your light shine." "Hate what is evil; hold fast to what is good." "Whatever is true, whatever is honorable . . . if there is any excellence . . . think about these things." "Pursue righteousness." "Remind them to be gentle." "Bear with one another." "Clothe yourselves with compassion, kindness, and humility. Above all, clothe yourselves with love." "Be imitators of God." "Strive first for the kingdom." "Restore transgressors in a spirit of gentleness." "Bear one another's burdens and so fulfill the law of Christ."

Toward the end of one particularly lovely burst of such hortatives, the apostle Paul turns directly to the topic that concerns us in this book, namely, how to find the confluence of wisdom and love as we help each other worship God:

> "For You are praised by the angels, archangels, thrones, dominions, principalities, authorities, powers, and the many-eyed Cherubim. Round about You stand the Seraphim. . . . Together with these blessed powers, loving Master, we sinners also cry out and say: Truly you are holy. . . ."
>
> The Divine Liturgy of St. Basil, trans. by Members of the Faculty of Hellenic College/Holy Cross Greek Orthodox School of Theology (Brookline, Mass.: Holy Cross Orthodox Press, 1988), pp. 24-25

2. E.g., Rom. 12:1-2, 9-21; Eph. 4:20–5:2; Phil. 2:1-4; Col. 3; 1 Thess. 5:12-22.

And let the peace of Christ rule in your hearts, to which indeed you were called in the one body. And be thankful. Let the word of Christ dwell in you richly; teach and admonish one another in all wisdom; and with gratitude in your hearts sing psalms, hymns, and spiritual songs to God. And whatever you do, in word or deed, do everything in the name of the Lord Jesus, giving thanks to God the Father through him. (Col. 3:15-17)

All this encouragement is for those who have been "raised with Christ" (Col. 3:1), and whose faith therefore rests not only in the person of Christ but also in his program of service and in the virtues that drive it. The person who trusts Jesus Christ, God's only Son, our Lord, therefore trusts (contrary to appearances and to Nietzsche) that kindness is a form of strength, and humility a species of wisdom. She trusts that obedience to God exalts a life instead of stifling it, and that a glad habit of listening to others, and lifting up their interests, can excite in a godly community a near-carnival of goodwill and self-irony.

In fact, the point of these guides for holy living is not first to tidy things up in our moral innards, desirable as such tidying may be, but to enable a whole community to thrive. A community with "peace in its heart" has room there as well for the Christ who gave it, and for the neighbor who needs it. In a peaceable kingdom we can know some of the songs of the heart, and can sing them with common enthusiasm for Jesus Christ and for his project in the world.

> *"The more clearly we learn to recognize that the ground and strength and promise of all our fellowship is in Jesus Christ alone, the more serenely shall we think of our fellowship and pray and hope for it."*
>
> Dietrich Bonhoeffer, *Life Together* (New York: Harper and Row, 1954), p. 31

Because of devotion to our common Lord, we may rejoice not only in our own salvation but also in the salvation of neighbors — who might express their worship, prayer, or joy in a way we wouldn't choose. A community of such peace allows us to teach each other, and even to "admonish" one another, secure in the faith that our teaching and admonition happen "in Christ," which means inside a cradle of grace. In such an environment, straight talk will be tempered by grace, and grace will retain its core of truth. Given our common goal of making God's heart glad, of thickening union with Christ, and of taking on nourishment for the cause of serving justice and pursuing peace in the world, we needn't nick each other's egos or threaten each other's partisan loyalties.

All this can sound utopian, but the amount of space devoted to prescribing it, or something like it, in these instructional sections of the New Testament tells us that Paul thought it was a normal goal of Christian life. Paul looks at factions, fighting, resentment, name-calling, belittling, and all the other features of church strife and says, simply, "Put it away." Put it to death. Don't *be* that way. Instead, forbear with each other, forgive one another, tell each other the truth in love, and, whatever you do — especially in the midst of your singing — give thanks to God in the name of Jesus Christ.

> "The habit of taking each other before God in prayer, familiarly and by name, is eminently beneficial. It will cleanse you. It will sweeten your disposition. It will take away from you every particle of the raven, that loves to feed on carrion."
>
> Henry Ward Beecher, from *Morning and Evening Exercises*

This will take small, medium, and large virtues in anyone who aspires to be even "a pretty good person," as Lewis Smedes describes her. To begin with, we'll need humility, one of the most underestimated virtues in the world. Yet all humility really requires is for one to be well-oriented to reality, which means remaining teachable, because no one person could possibly "know it all," and also remaining reachable, because no one in the church should presume to be the stoic, heroic Lone Ranger.

We'll need candor, or verbal straightforwardness. This, in fact, is a type of justice because it precludes hidden agendas and cloaked daggers. The point is to face each other squarely so we know where the other stands, because only then can we deal with each other at the level of real concerns.

We'll need hospitality, the gracious readiness to make room for others and their interests. This does not mean that we simply relinquish our own identity, but rather that we look for ways in which our identity is actually enriched by accepting, welcoming, and entertaining that of others. Self-assured hospitality means we'll be open-minded (but not so open-minded that our brains fall out, as Ann Landers once quipped).

We'll need forbearance: the willingness to put up with people who make us crazy. Sometimes this means tolerating others' interests, which has nothing to do with fostering a blandly neutral outlook. Instead it has to do with putting up with something you don't want for the sake of something bigger that you do want.[3]

"Over all these things," of course, we'll need to "put on love" (cf. Col. 3:14), which is a many-splendored garment, but which for present purposes may be defined as simple goodwill toward our neighbor, a desire to see her flourish as God intended.

When the apostle Paul writes of these things in his letters, he writes to churches that are divided or that are in danger of division, and he calls their members to renew the image of God by such means as telling the truth, putting away their anger after a time, working hard *in order* to have something to give to those who have less, and adopting a tenderhearted attitude toward sinners. The idea is that to do these things is to be like God. To act like this is to act like God. More specifically, to act like this is to represent Jesus Christ, the preeminent image of God the Father (2 Cor. 4:4; Col. 1:15). We image God by imaging Christ, and we image Christ by showing godly knowledge, righteousness, and holiness (Eph. 4:24; Col. 3: 10). Candor, hospitality, and forbearance are just ways of spelling out righteousness. Accordingly, for an ordinary Christian in an ordinary Christian community it should be an awesome thing to consider that

> *"Hope is a projection of the imagination;*
> * so is despair.*
> *Despair all too readily embraces*
> * the ills it foresees;*
> *hope is an energy and arouses the mind*
> * to every possibility to combat*
> * them. . . ."*
>
> Thornton Wilder, cited by Eugene Peterson in *A Long Obedience in the Same Direction*, p. 132

3. J. Budziszewski, *True Tolerance: Liberalism and the Necessity of Judgment* (New Brunswick: Transaction, 1992), p. 7.

every time she struggles to deal patiently with a way of worshiping that seems to her boring, or obnoxious, she is imaging God. She is both expressing and strengthening her union with Christ.

Considerations of this kind help us to see the "holy living" sections of Scripture in the same way as we see the church, namely, as a part of the gospel and not as a mere addendum to it. The reason is that these sections present us with the counsels of grace by the God of grace who knows how life flourishes in union with Christ and wishes to share the recipe. God's commands orient us to covenant living and tell us how to make it sing. It is part of Karl Barth's enduring spiritual genius to see this truth and to insist upon it. God's command is "the form of the gospel" that invites "joyful participation" in good life with God and each other. God's call to compassion, for example, is itself compassionate. When we refuse God's commands, it's grace we are refusing. It's freedom we are refusing. We think we are refusing a bad death, but we are actually refusing the good death that leads to resurrection and life.[4] "The good command of God," writes Otto Weber, comes to us not out of pique, and not out of the blue, but "in Christ," "in the Lord Jesus," "by the name of our Lord Jesus Christ," "by the mercies of God." From Barth and Weber's writing we might come to a healthy conclusion: forget about "principles," "duties," and even "virtues," if you must, and let your Christian ethics amount to "thought-out parenetics" in which indicative mercy gets transformed into imperative mercy[5] — and not the least in the area of worship, where rancor appears not only divisive but also absurd.

With respect to worship, it is time (once more) to try to move the discussion forward. In fact, it's high noon. The reason is that troubled churches can't pursue their mission in the world very well. Rancor saps a church's energy and distracts its attention from God.

So the main project in this book is to set a context and recom-

---

4. Karl Barth, *Church Dogmatics,* trans. G. W. Bromiley, ed. G. W. Bromiley and T. F. Torrance, vol. 2 (Edinburgh: T&T Clark, 1957), pp. 579, 581.

5. Otto Weber, *Foundations of Dogmatics,* vol. 2, trans. Darrell L. Guder (Grand Rapids: Eerdmans, 1983), pp. 342, 402, 406.

mend a tone in which healthy decisions about worship may be conducted. Though we think the church always needs prophets, we will not offer a simple jeremiad against Contemporary Worship. After all, it has new strengths and vitalities, and we need them. But neither will we accept uncritically every novelty that churches try in their attempt to be modern, relevant, with-it. What we hope instead is to offer help in making discerning choices about worship in an era of remarkable change in North America and beyond.

We begin in Chapter Two with a travelogue of sorts, a survey of worship practices in North America, looking especially at the Contemporary Worship scene, but not exclusively so. Easily asked questions defy easy answers. This is no less true of the question "What is Contemporary Worship?" than of "Who is God?" So we've deliberately attempted to "complexify" the answer to that first question, not least in order to widen our view of the Christian church today.

"Complexifying" is a tactic we take up in the third chapter, too, where we raise questions about Christ and culture with respect to worship. What does it mean to be *in* the world though not *of* it, and how should we make that plain in the way we worship? Here again, we cannot pretend that there are easy answers to every question and every situation. But even if there are no easy answers, this doesn't mean there are *no* answers. That, too, would be pretense. We are left to wrestle for the truth and often against our inclinations.

But this struggle, as we'll see, isn't something we take up in isolation, either as individual church leaders or as independent congregations. The struggle is communal, the effort of a body, made up of many members but submitted to a single head. So in Chapter Four we examine this body, its diversity and its unity. We explore our fellowship as believers, discovering along the way that it is the divine fellowship of the Trinity that makes sense of our oneness even as it invites us to embrace our many-ness.

In Chapter Five we look for how this is so in the church while it worships. Questions that come to the fore in this chapter include the very nature of worship, the drama it enacts, and the hope that it manifests.

Chapter 2

Costa Mesa, South Barrington, and Rome: The Rise of Contemporary Worship

ANY GIVEN SUNDAY IN GINGHAMSBURG CHURCH, Tipp City, Ohio, the auditorium lights will dim and a giant projection screen will flicker. At Ginghamsburg, worship incorporates multimedia modules that resemble late-night TV talk shows, major network comedies, or local rock radio. One week it may be a David Letterman-esque "Top Ten Ways to Know You're in a Bad Church." Another week a service about forgiveness may peak with the band's performance of Don Henley's "The Heart of the Matter." Or maybe the theme *du jour* will be introduced with a parody of cable TV's *Food Network:* Chef Gucciano is presented "'live' via satellite" as he extols the virtues of a few good spices to titillate our taste buds — and what was it Jesus said about salt?[1]

Any given Sunday, the music of a worship band, children's choir, or organ may welcome those who enter the sanctuary of Shepherd of the Valley Presbyterian Church, Albuquerque, New Mexico. After this prelude, the worship — the same at 8:00, 9:30, and 11:00 — proceeds according to a printed order of service recommended by the

---

1. Illustrations taken from Michael Slaughter, *Out on the Edge: A Wake-up Call for Church Leaders on the Edge of the Media Reformation* (Nashville: Abingdon, 1998), book and CD ROM; and Ginghamsburg, "Call to Worship," copyright © 1997-2001 Ginghamsburg Church, http://www.ginghamsburg.org/bookstor/callwp98.htm (30 April 2001).

denomination. The sermon's theme is based on the liturgical season, and the drama (written by a member of the staff) and the music are, in turn, based on the sermon. Because of the ethnic diversity of the congregation, worshipers expect to sing, pray, hear Scripture, and receive blessing sometimes in English, sometimes in Spanish.[2]

Any given Sunday, the Gothic arches and vaulted ceiling of St. Augustine Roman Catholic Church in Washington, D.C., will swell with the trap set chatter, bass guitar riffs, and electric organ vibe of a black gospel groove. Robed in white, members of the choir more than process to their loft: they sway and dance, clap and sing, while above their four-, five-, sometimes six-part harmony a trumpet and saxophone may produce ripping improvisations that stretch for the stratosphere.[3]

Any given Sunday, worship leaders at Willow Creek Community Church in South Barrington, Illinois, will treat those who've gathered as "those who are checking out what it really means to have a personal relationship with Jesus." Contemporary music performed by a semi-professional band; a drama presented by well-rehearsed actors; a message delivered with straight, highly illustrative rhetoric and maybe a video clip or two; a clear invitation not to put money in the collection plate — these and every other element of Willow Creek's Sunday morning ministry are designed to open the door of faith to "seekers," who are welcome to merely listen and observe. If and when they've crossed the threshold of faith, then they're invited to become participants in a midweek New Community service. There, the actions of worship might share the same look and the same sound, but the service is planned for believers, not for seekers.[4]

2. Samuel D. Perriccioli, "Worship Leader Profile: Unity in Diversity," *Worship Leader* 8, no. 5 (September/October 1999): 28-30, 32.

3. David Parks (producer), *Fire in the Pews* (Belleville, Ill.: Oblate Media and Communication Corporation, 1987).

4. Willow Creek Community Church, "More About Willow Creek: Services," copyright © 1999, http://www.willowcreek.org/Services.htm (30 April 2001); Lynne Hybels and Bill Hybels, "A Mission and a Strategy," chap. 11 in *Rediscovering Church: The Story and Vision of Willow Creek Community Church* (Grand Rapids: Zondervan, 1995); Bill Hybels et al., *An Inside Look at the Willow Creek Seeker Service: Show Me the Way* (South Barrington, Ill., and Grand Rapids, Mich.: Zondervan Video, 1992).

Any given Sunday, in San Antonio, Texas, thousands of Mexican Americans will gather for worship. Among them, some will "enter into the presence of the Lord" through the praise and worship ministry of Iglesia Bethel, where a live band leads one of the city's largest Spanish-speaking congregations.[5] Nearer the heart of San Antonio, parishioners at Mission San José Church will participate in a colorful mariachi Mass.[6] Here, psalms, hymns, and service music are set to the syncopated rhythms of Mexican *jarabes* (dances) and *corridos* (ballads), led by a mariachi ensemble of trumpets, violins, a six-stringed *guitarrón*, and a five-stringed *vihuela.*

Any given Sunday, a hundred-some folk will step off the sidewalk into the storefront sanctuary that is Solomon's Porch in Minneapolis, Minnesota. They have come for an evening Worship Gathering, so named because "service" is such a confusing term: just who is being "served"? The ceiling is low, and so is the lighting. Candles and incandescent lamps illumine a motley, semicircular arrangement of couches, armchairs, and coffee tables around a braided rug. Each wall is painted a different bold color, and each is graced with artwork. Solomon's Porch is intended to be "a place for people seeking a fresh approach to Faith, Spirituality, and Historical Christianity." So worship itself is an interspersion of songs, all of which are original to their band; prayers, which may be extemporaneous or read from ancient texts; Scripture readings; personal narratives; a pastoral reflection on a biblical passage; silent contemplation; and Communion.[7]

Any given Sunday, millions of people will gather in churches established more than one hundred years ago in denominations established more than three hundred years ago. Many of these believers will enter a sanctuary in silence, quietly awaiting a choral introit. Some will stand

5. Iglesia Bethel, "Pastor's Welcome Message" and "Praise and Worship Ministry," copyright © 1999, http://www.iglesiabethel.org (30 April 2001).

6. Mission San José, "The 'Queen of the Missions,'" http://sanjosemission.com (30 April 2001).

7. Solomon's Porch, "Homepage," http://www.solomonsporch.com (18 January 2001). In June, 2002, Solomon's Porch began meeting in a new location. The description of their worship and commitment to community remains the same (http://www.solomonsporch.com, 1 August 2003).

to sing four-part harmony from a four-pound hymnbook. Others will read a psalm responsively, perhaps interposed with a sung refrain. In several churches, those who have gathered will offer silent prayers of confession after which they will receive an assurance of God's pardon. They will listen to the lectionary texts and respond "Thanks be to God" when the reader concludes with "The Word of the Lord." They will hear a thoughtful sermon, recite the Apostles' Creed, and celebrate the Lord's Supper. In some churches, they might even circle-dance around the Table. Throughout the year, they will observe not just Christmas, Good Friday, and Easter, but Advent, Epiphany, and Lent as well.

Any given Sunday, worship takes shape in a variety of ways, in a variety of communities, for a variety of reasons. A generation ago, the scenario in the last paragraph might have fit as many as three of every four worshiping communities gathered in North America on Sunday mornings. Today, it's still an apt description for many, though for fewer than before. During the last several decades, Christian worship has been diversifying in North America, at a rate and reach seemingly greater than that which succeeded even the Reformation. And it's a diversifying that knows few bounds — that is to say, it is readily found among denominations and nondenominations, in mega-churches and micro-churches, in the metropolis, the suburbs, and the countryside.

WHY SO MANY CHANGES?

During the last several decades, particular movements have been pushing churches in new directions, giving them whole new modes of expression, most obviously in worship.

For instance, the church growth movement is one of the primary motivating forces behind churches like Ginghamsburg and Willow Creek.[8] Since the mid 1970s and the early 1980s, this movement has

8. While conducting Willow Creek's first-ever church leadership conference in Germany (November 1996), Bill Hybels expressed a qualified association with the church

given North Americans a fresh conception of church and worship. Under its influence, church leaders, compelled to seek and to save the lost through worship, have undertaken the task of making their congregation's service accessible to those who are not yet Christians, an intent that affects not just what is presented but also how it's presented. Adopting a principle something like a mass-marketing technique — namely, the hotly debated, sociologically founded "homogeneous unit principle"[9] — proponents of the church growth movement commend liturgical events targeted to particular audiences, often defined by the status of their faith (seekers or believers), by their age group (Boomers, Busters, Gen-Xers, or, most recently, Millennials), by their cultural background, or by a combination of these three. Theorists of the church growth movement capitalize on economic and cultural idioms to put forth their ideas, which is why we read of a congregation's "market niche," and why we find worship resources published under titles like *Net Results* or *Entertainment Evangelism*.[10]

> "We describe Willow Creek as being a safe place where seekers can hear the very dangerous, life-changing message of Jesus Christ."
>
> Bill and Lynne Hybels, *Rediscovering Church* (Grand Rapids: Zondervan, 1995), p. 206

While the church growth movement is one of the motivating forces behind churches like Ginghamsburg and Willow Creek, it is by no means the only force. In the late 1960s, a series of revivals swept the nation. Given their resemblance to the pentecostal outpourings of a half-century prior, these revivals became known as the charismatic movement, and nearly every Christian tradition has been

---

growth movement: "There has been a church-growth movement which is primarily preoccupied with increased attendance. We at Willow Creek are concerned about much more than just attendance." See Bill Yoder, "Hybels Does Hamburg: Will Willow Creek's Model Float in Germany?" *Christianity Today* 41, no. 1 (6 January 1997): 61.

9. This principle was championed especially by Donald A. McGavran, founding dean of the School of World Mission at Fuller Theological Seminary, 1965. See McGavran, *Understanding Church Growth* (Grand Rapids: Eerdmans, 1970, 1980, and 1990).

10. Tom Bandy, senior editor, http://www.netresults.org (1 August 2003); also Walt Kallestad, *Entertainment Evangelism* (Nashville: Abingdon, 1996).

Church Attenders as Worship Consumers: Point and Counterpoint
Lester Ruth

Join the conversation about the role of the church in North American culture. How should the church respond to a consumerist culture? Should we protest all use of consumer categories? Should we market the church in ways that advance the gospel? Or is there a third way that maintains a delicate balance, remaining "in, but not of" our culture? Below are two representative voices to open up the discussion. Robb Redman's "The Commercial Connection" (in Chapter Three) might further it.

Timothy Wright, *A Community of Joy: How to Create Contemporary Worship* (Nashville: Abingdon, 1994).

"The generations after 1946 have forever changed the way people choose churches."

"People now choose churches in much the same way they make all other choices — as consumers (not necessarily as believers). They go where the action is — where they think their needs will be met — regardless of denomination, apparent doctrine, or location."

"For consumers, the worship service is one of the major reasons for choosing a church. Because they value worship style, most shoppers visit several churches before making their decision."

"For congregations committed to reaching new people, the implications warrant serious consideration: Attracting and reaching the unchurched means a thorough and sympathetic understanding of their unique values and motivations. It means seeing life and church through their eyes. It means designing worship services that correspond to their needs and values."

"Not all the values that guests bring to worship are compatible with Christianity; nor are such values confined solely to the irreligious. Believers also embrace some of these same values as they shop for a church home. However, in order to effectively reach new people, congregations must find ways to attract their attention. By creatively responding to consumer values, without compromising integrity, churches can impact people with the gospel."

Philip D. Kenneson, "Selling [Out] the Church in the Marketplace of Desire," *Modern Theology* 9, no. 4 (October 1993): 319-48.

"One problem with such marketing approaches is that they misname those challenges and problems facing contemporary churches in America. The management fix offered by the church marketers, focused as it must be on matters of church life that are measurable and controllable, cannot address the real problems facing churches, not the least of which is their deep confusion about the church's identity and purpose. It would seem to do little good to offer techniques for encouraging churches to grow while leaving unexplored more basic questions, such as: Who are we as a church? . . ."

"Once a church allows its identity to be transfigured into one more forum for mutually beneficial exchanges between producers and consumers, an entirely new set of questions arise that frame ecclesial thought and practice. For example, within such a scheme, who are the producers and who are the consumers? In practice, the clergy are often identified as producers and the laity as consumers, thereby creating a division with the body of Christ as insidious as any medieval ecclesiastical hierarchy. . . . Or if the 'unchurched' are the consumers and the 'churched' are producers, at what point and by what means does one's orientation change from one to the other?"

"But what the church marketers fail to realize is that their very choice to employ marketing strategies has already reshaped the field, including the 'product.' . . . Much that is central to the Christian life will not fit neatly into the management/marketing scheme, and not surprisingly, these matters never seem to be addressed by church marketers. In effect, the 'good news' has been filtered through a rather fine marketing sieve, the result being that many of the less marketable claims which God has on our lives have been removed, leaving for the consumer those aspects of the Christian faith most readily translated into terms of self-interest."

warmed by its fire. Just scan the church ads in a local newspaper and consider how many worshiping communities offer invitations to "an authentic experience of God through Spirit-filled worship."

When associated with worship, words like "authentic" and "experience" are perhaps the most obvious signs of the charismatic movement's radiant heat. But there are others. In churches of every denomination and nondenomination, we find worshipers who sway their bodies, raise their hands, close their eyes, and turn their faces to the heavens. While someone preaches or prays, they respond with shouts of praise or hums of approval. Theirs is something of a pentecostal expectation: who knows what might happen when the power of God is "called down" and the Holy Spirit lights fire in our hearts?[11]

Closely related to the charismatic movement is the praise-and-worship movement (it might be thought of as a second-generation direct descendant). Because of P&W, a distinct pattern of worship has been espoused not only in Pentecostal churches but in several mainline churches as well: vigorous praise prepares the hearts of worshipers for contemplative intimacy with God; fast-paced rhythms and vocal fervor settle down to soulful melodies and quiet ecstasy. Accordingly, worship leaders will invite worshipers to "enter his gates with thanksgiving and his courts with praise" with songs like "He Has Made Me Glad," and then invite them to "enter into the presence of God" with songs such as "I Love You, Lord" and "Lord, You're Beautiful."

Proponents of P&W have generated a thriving industry, complete with published music, copyright licensing procedures, tapes and CDs, books and magazines, manuals and conferences. The reach of this industry, and thus this movement, is long, evidenced by the fact that P&W's Scripture songs (like Marty Nystrom's "As the Deer") and praise choruses (like Rick Founds's "Lord, I Lift Your

---

11. For a further exposition, consider David di Sabatino, "The Unforgettable Fire: Pentecostals and the Role of Experience in Worship," *Worship Leader* 9, no. 6 (November/December 2000): 20-23.

Name on High") have found their place on the projection screens or printed liturgies of evangelical and mainline churches alike, no matter what their ethnic background or their cultural milieu. With little effort, one can search the Internet and find P&W songs translated for every nation and tribe, language and people: Portuguese, Spanish, Vietnamese, Mandarin, Korean, Japanese, and on around the globe, as far as one's imagination wants to trot. Often these translations are associated with ethnic minority congregations in North America. Such churches may conduct worship in their first language, with or without English translation; or they may offer multiple services, one in a first language and another in English; or their ministry may be English only. In any case, the sounds of Contemporary Worship have found so warm a welcome in many of these worshiping communities that, for example, at the Website of a church such as The Ascension English Ministry of the Los Angeles Korean United Methodist Church in California, one may find reviews and purchasing access for music as diverse as the praise and worship of WoW,[12] the R&B of CeCe Winans, the retro-swing of The W's, and the alternative rock of the British band Delirious?.[13] Furthermore, P&W praise-song collections are now being published not only by Maranatha! or Integrity Music but also by Augsburg Fortress Press, whose *Worship and Praise Songbook* came out in 1999.

So the church growth, charismatic, and praise-and-worship movements, taken together, help to account for the worship settings of churches like Ginghamsburg, Willow Creek, and Iglesia Bethel.

---

12. These CDs are generated jointly by the big-three worship music publishing houses: Maranatha!, Vineyard Music Group, and Integrity Music. From the WoW Worship website FAQ: "What does 'WoW' stand for? Some of the best times being a Christian are WoW Worship Moments; those lump-in-the-throat, indescribable times when God shows up. They can make you sing, dance or cry. WoW is in actuality, the overwhelming presence of God. What can you say but WoW?" ("WoW" Worship Frequently Asked Questions, © 2001 Integrity Incorporated, http://www.wowworship.com/faq.html [12 July 2002]).

13. Ascension Ministry, "Music Store," http://www.ascensionministry.org/music.htm (12 July 2002).

African American Worship

Melva Wilson Costen

Although African Americans share many common worship practices, one should not assume that *all* African American congregations will or should exhibit homogenous styles of worship. Different situations and circumstances under which exposure to Christianity took place for each congregation, denomination (history and theological orientation), geography, and social lifestyles are significant determinants of worship.

The traditional manner of "labeling" denominational differences among African American worshipers has not always been accurate, nor has it been helpful. The stereotyping of ritual action has not always taken into consideration the sociological factors of cross ritual assimilation *between* denominations, especially in small communities in the South. There are also differences in ritual action *within* denominations. To assume, for instance, that all African American Presbyterians should be numbered among the "frozen-chosen" is to ignore the dynamics of "Spirit-filled" churches such as those in rural sections of North and South Carolina and Georgia. To claim that *all* African American Baptist worship services are highly emotional is to negate the "modulated" liturgical experiences and expressions of *some* African American Baptists in both urban and rural settings. The trend from the late sixties forward among some African American congregations traditionally labeled "frozen," "staid," or "unemotional" has been toward a more expressive worship. Some African American Catholic, Episcopalian, United Methodist, Disciples of Christ, United Church of

---

Those who pay attention to the worship scene in North America would agree that these churches, as outcomes of these movements, epitomize Contemporary Worship. In the minds of many, that pair of words evokes the sounds of amplified drums, guitars, keyboards, and voices; it evokes images of dimmed auditoriums, a spotlit stage, and projected lyrics.

While these movements figure prominently in the worship of churches like Ginghamsburg, Willow Creek, and Iglesia Bethel, they also explain features of worship at churches like St. Augustine and Shepherd of the Valley. The telltale signs? Guitars and gospel music, drama and praise songs. But other movements are afoot in these last two churches, too, and we do well to track them since they are not without influence in the Contemporary Worship of churches like Ginghamsburg and Willow Creek.

Christ, Lutheran, and Presbyterian worshipers are rediscovering and reclaiming their common Afro-centric theological roots. . . .

The genius of Black worship is its openness to the creative power of God that frees and enables people, regardless of denomination, to "turn themselves loose" and celebrate God's act in Jesus Christ. In the process, worshipers are inspired to be creative. Indeed, traditional African American worship can be viewed as a spiritual art form. The drama inherent in worship lends itself naturally to joyful glorification and enjoyment of God. This is *not* to say that *all* Black worship is designed to be entertaining, nor are all worship experiences filled with physical excitement. Stereotyping of worship undermines mission and ministry, so important in the Black community. There *is* a balance in African American worship forms that is most often identi-

fied by denominational distinctions and geographical differences.

Much more has been written and confirmed about traditional African American denominations than about African American congregations in Euro-American denominations. It is true that African American denominations have been a major stabilizing force in the Black community. Nevertheless, the term "Black church" also includes African American congregations functioning separately from their Euro-American parent churches. To overlook any African American contributors to social change and liturgical life severs the inherent unity of African Americans wherever they find themselves.

Excerpts from *African American Christian Worship* (Nashville: Abingdon, 1993), pp. 15-16 and 77-78.

In large part, Mission San José and St. Augustine Roman Catholic Church worship as they do because of Vatican II, summoned in the early 1960s by Pope John XXIII. Asked about his intentions for this council, the Pope once walked to a window, threw it open, and let in a draft of fresh air.[14] Standing in the council's breeze, the Pope, and the entire world with him, watched as significant changes overcame the church, not least in its worship. Deemed esoteric and out-of-touch with the modern world, Roman Catholic rites, declared the council, "should be distinguished by a noble simplicity."[15] This meant that services would be simplified, ostentatious vestments

14. This according to "T.B.McD.," "The Second Vatican Council for Catholic Students," http://www.christusrex.org/www1/CDHN/v1.html (1 August 2003).

15. *Sacrosanctum Concilium (Constitution on the Sacred Liturgy),* Second Vatican Council, 4 December 1963, III.D.34.

closeted, and Latin shelved. In native tongue, people would sing psalms, hymns, and spiritual songs, accompanied not necessarily by a pipe organ but by whatever instrument seemed fitting for the culture and the occasion.[16] "Even in the liturgy the Church does not wish to impose a rigid uniformity in matters which do not involve the faith or the good of the whole community," declared the council, and so the church resolved to "respect and foster the qualities and talents of the various races and nations."[17]

As a result, bishoprics, wherever they're located, have been urged to find a liturgical expression that conveys the church's teachings while reflecting local color. So Catholics in Waterford, Ireland, might sing the Mass accompanied by a fiddle, a penny-whistle, and a Celtic drum,[18] while Catholics in Kinshasa, Zaire, dressed in colorful batik vestments, might circle-dance around the altar in patterned steps to the rhythms of African hand drums.[19] And then there are the African-American Catholics at St. Augustine in the northwest quadrant of Washington, D.C., who with their Caucasian brothers and sisters celebrate Mass in a black gospel groove; and the Mexican-American Catholics at the Mission San José in south central Texas who recite the creed in Spanish and sing the Kyrie to a soulful *corrido.*

This popularization and contextualization of worship is common among the progeny not only of Vatican II but also of the church growth movement, and it's the former that has influenced the latter, if only indirectly. Throughout the last generation, historians have observed that Protestants, especially those in mainline denominations, have experienced greater changes in their worship because of Vatican II than many Catholics have experienced. So the longing at Ginghamsburg — a United Methodist ministry — to provide "a

---

16. *Sacrosanctum Concilium,* IV.120.

17. *Sacrosanctum Concilium,* III.D.37.

18. Soon after Vatican II, Fintan O'Carroll and several colleagues in Ireland established the Irish Church Music Association, whose aim was to compose music that was distinctly Irish and aesthetically worthy for use in worship.

19. Thomas A. Kane, *The Dancing Church: Video Impressions of the Church in Africa* (Mahwah, N.J.: Paulist, 1991), videorecording.

Hispanic Worship

Justo L. González

Hispanic worship has many faces. . . . Think, for instance, of a Mexican Roman Catholic parish composed mostly of persons who prefer to worship in Spanish and who still have deep roots in Mexican culture. In that parish, the Mass will be central, probably in Spanish with mariachi music, and perhaps even some liturgical dances patterned after ancient Mexican dances. . . .

In the same neighborhood there may be a Pentecostal church whose doctrine is staunchly anti-Roman Catholic but whose members come from the same strata of society as the majority of those in the Catholic church. Instead of the Mass, their worship will center on preaching, praise, *testimonios, coritos* [simple refrains sung by heart], and prayer for healing. The *coritos,* however, will most likely be sung to the accompaniments of a mariachi-style band, rather than Caribbean-style maracas and drums. . . . In the same community, there may be a "mainline" Protestant church whose worship is mostly in English and follows the general pattern of Anglo churches of the same denomina-

tions. Still, when they celebrate a baptism they do so with a number of elements unknown in Anglo congregations, but quite common in the Mexican tradition — godparents, special dresses and foods, and practices of *compadrazgo* [co-parents]. In that same church, there may be a time set aside during the worship service for *coritos,* and they may also sing some songs taken from the mariachi Mass normally sung down the street. Meanwhile, at the other end of the country, in New York, similar combinations are taking place, although in a different context since the Mexican influence is not as powerful as the Puerto Rican or Dominican.

. . . There are a number of churches — relatively few, and mostly very small — whose membership is mostly Latinos and Latinas but whose worship is scarcely distinguishable from what takes place at eleven o'clock in predominantly Anglo congregations of the same denomination. . . .

In brief, there are many faces to Hispanic worship, and any attempt to describe that worship without taking that variety into consideration would be false.

Excerpts from *¡Alabadle!: Hispanic Christian Worship* (Nashville: Abingdon, 1996), pp. 12-14.

---

relevant and contemporary setting for worship"[20] is owed, in part, to Vatican inspiration. And so is Shepherd of the Valley's, and so is Willow Creek's, and so is yours.

Two more words about Vatican II. First, Vatican II's move toward the inculturation of worship has contributed to a global move

20. Ginghamsburg, "Who We Are," copyright © 1997-2001 Ginghamsburg Church, http://www.ginghamsburg.org/whoweare/welcome.htm (30 April 2001).

toward cross-culturation of worship. From around the world, worshiping traditions are sharing their melodies and rhythms and the musical instruments that authenticate their sound. In the last thirty years, denominational hymnbooks and their supplements have proliferated in North America, nearly every one of which includes worship songs transcribed in ethnic communities either here or abroad. Several denominational publishers have begun producing hymnals for their ethnic minority congregations, but these minority congregations are not their only market. Many worship planners and church musicians, like those at Shepherd of the Valley, are looking for resources to enrich their worship with cultural variety.

Second, nurtured by an especially Roman Catholic interest in historic patterns of Christian worship, a liturgical movement has taken root among even Protestant churches in North America, and it has yielded an impressive harvest. Never before have the worship books of mainline denominations looked so similar. Because of this movement, Mennonites and Brethren are forming lectionary study groups, Presbyterians and Methodists are singing their Eucharistic prayers, and evangelicals are lighting Advent candles.

Recognizing these movements, along with their overlapping spheres of influence, is one way to account for the diversity of worship found in North American churches today. No matter how it might be labeled, whatever worship takes place this coming Sunday — whether in the sanctuary of First Community, Second Baptist, Third Reformed, or Fourth Presbyterian, or at the altar of St. Peter's Orthodox, St. Paul's Lutheran, or St. Mary's Catholic — that worship is contemporary, current, of the present period. But, then, there is also little dispute that a distinct form of worship has developed in the last half century, and that it has been labeled "Contemporary Worship" — capital C, capital W — by inside planners and outside observers alike.

Since Contemporary Worship is the substance of this chapter, indeed, of this book, we turn our attention solely to this form of present-day worship. But we do well to be reminded, as we were at the outset of this discussion and will be again at its end, that Contemporary Worship is only one among many forms of present-day worship, albeit a prominent one.

A BACKWARD GLANCE

To begin exploring Contemporary Worship, we might find it helpful to keep our backward glance, looking not just at a few movements in the church that have fostered Contemporary Worship but also at a history of Contemporary Worship itself. Like many phenomena in history, it's not as though one can name a date and an event and say, "This. This marked its beginning." No, like other phenomena, Contemporary Worship evolved. It evolved not only out of the movements already named, but also from the force of a number of historical events and influential personalities.[21]

Already in the 1940s and 50s, something new was emerging in American Protestantism because of the evangelistic zeal of visionaries like Torrey Johnson, Billy Graham, Jim Rayburn, and Bill Bright. While American troops combated communism abroad, these evangelists' para-church youth ministries countered atheism at home. At early Youth for Christ rallies, says Graham, "snappy Gospel music, interesting testimonies, and (most of all) short, youth-oriented sermons combined to attract thousands of lonely, insecure, and frightened teenagers and young adults."[22] While Graham attempted to reach young people through large-scale rallies, another evangelical minister, Jim Rayburn, attempted to reach them through friendships and household gatherings, and, in 1941 in Gainsville, Texas, Young Life was born. Clubs soon proliferated throughout the country. "Painstakingly tailored to teenage concepts" — their vernacular, their values,

---

21. For this history, we are indebted to the input of Robb Redman, a member of our discussion group, and Chuck Fromm, editor of *Worship Leader* magazine.

22. Billy Graham, *Just As I Am: The Autobiography of Billy Graham* (San Francisco: HarperSanFrancisco/Zondervan, 1997), p. 92.

their venue — Young Life's weekly gatherings, like Graham's rallies, featured popular music (sacred and secular), "floor shows" (skits and comedy routines), and a winsome presentation of an equally winsome Christ. The simple intent was (and is) to introduce Christ, and to put no pressure on teens to accept him or to join a church.[23]

By 1960, Youth for Christ, Young Life, Campus Crusade, and other ministries like them were generating a growing repertoire of songs and choruses set to pop tunes to attract and hold the attention of what was becoming an increasingly estranged youth culture. By the time Baby Boomers had come of high school and college age in the sixties, the piano had become passé and the guitar vogue, in part because guitars were portable, and in part because they were popular.

> "Rather than passive acceptance of, and accommodation to, diverging generational cultures, the religious community is challenged to exercise agency, defining and forging an inclusive world of meaning and practice that bridges those boundaries."
>
> Jackson W. Carroll and Wade Clark Roof, *Bridging Divided Worlds* (San Francisco: Jossey-Bass, 2002), p. 13

During the sixties and into the seventies, the Southern gospel tunes and testimonial lyrics of Bill and Gloria Gaither were making their mark within the church and without. Inspired by a revival meeting experience near Alexandria, Indiana, "He Touched Me" was the Gaither Trio's first hit. Published in 1963 and almost immediately recorded by other gospel artists, it was soon played on the radio as often as it was sung in churches. In 1969, Elvis Presley's rendition rose near the top of the Top-40 and received a Grammy nomination.

On another gospel front, musicians in African-American communities had developed a fresh voice of their own. For decades, jazz riffs and blues notes had been accompanying worship in black Baptist, Methodist, and charismatic churches, not least because of the influence of Thomas Dorsey. During the 1950s and early 1960s, James

---

23. See especially chaps. 1 and 2 of Emile Cailliet, *Young Life* (New York: Harper and Row, 1963). See also Ronald C. White Jr., "Youth Ministry at the Center: A Case Study of Young Life," in *Re-Forming the Center: American Protestantism: 1900 to the Present* (Grand Rapids: Eerdmans, 1998), pp. 361-80.

Cleveland's elaborately robed choirs produced "the ideal sound in gospel," though an undercurrent of harder sounds was rapidly flowing into the churches because of black gospel's emergence in the popular market.[24] In 1969, the same year as the Gaither-Presley hit, Edwin Hawkins and his Northern Carolina Youth State Choir produced another with their juiced up version of a gospel favorite, "Oh, Happy Day."

And then there were the Jesus People. Disillusioned by both the psychedelia of the sixties and the established church of the centuries, devout "hippies" fashioned a new and charismatic expression of evangelical Christianity

> *"We began worship with nothing but a sense of calling from the Lord to a deeper relationship with him."*
>
> Carol Wimber, cited in John Wimber, "Worship: Intimacy with God," http://www.vineyardboise.org/specialized_ministries/worship/ wimber_worship.htm (18 July 2002)

that (ironically) "established" itself during the early 1970s in communities such as Calvary Chapel, Costa Mesa, California.[25] In 1971, Tommy Coomes and his band Love Song, along with several other Calvary Chapel musicians, produced a recording, *The Everlastin' Living Jesus Music Concert*. That album, sold from the trunks of cars, marked the beginning of Maranatha! Music, the foremost publishing and recording company of praise-and-worship songs and choruses generated by the Jesus Movement and beyond.[26] In 1973, Maranatha! produced another record, *The Praise Album*, and by 1977 twenty-nine more.

Signature sounds of the Jesus Movement run the gamut from Karen Lafferty's "Seek Ye First" to Larry Norman's "The Rock That Doesn't Roll." Music from Lafferty's end of the continuum was particularly influential in the praise-and-worship genre of worship, while music from Norman's end was related to the growth of yet another influential "industry," namely, Christian Contemporary Music

24. Horace Clarence Boyer, *The Golden Age of Gospel* (Chicago: University of Illinois Press, 2000), pp. 257-58.

25. See "The Hip Church" in R. Enroth et al., *The Jesus People: Old-Time Religion in the Age of Aquarius* (Grand Rapids: Eerdmans, 1972).

26. Steve Rabey, "Maranatha! Music Comes of Age," *Christianity Today* 35, no. 5 (9 April 1991): 44-45, 47.

(CCM®).[27] Some of the industry's musicians — such as Amy Grant and Michael W. Smith — achieved crossover status in the secular market, not unlike many of their gospel music forebears, while other musicians — such as the late Keith Green, the late Rich Mullins, Michael Card, and Twila Paris — stepped in another direction, producing songs more clearly intended for worship. More recently, industry insider Charlie Peacock has pushed a prophetic edge, calling the entire CCM community, standing *At the Crossroads,* to account for its ways and means, and to expand its kingdom perspective for a fresh understanding of Christian music.[28]

During the 1970s and early 1980s, says C. Peter Wagner of Fuller Theological Seminary, North America experienced a "Third Wave" of charismatic movements.[29] Riding the crest of that wave was Vineyard Christian Fellowship (VCF), not least because of the charismatic zeal of one-time rocker John Wimber.[30] Like the Costa Mesa–based Calvary Chapel, VCF soon spawned its own recording and publishing house, Mercy Records (1984), which has since been named the Vineyard Music Group (VMG). Keeping stride with VMG is Integrity Music (1988), yet another publishing and recording house established by a consortium of smaller charismatic churches. While publishing houses abound, what really makes their music accessible is the copyright clearinghouse Christian Copyright Licensing, Inc., or CCLI, which handles royalty payments to subscribing copyright holders on behalf of CCLI's license holders; for this service, the license holders (nearly 120,000 churches and organizations in the United States

27. The acronym CCM is a registered trademark of CCM Communications.

28. Charlie Peacock, *At the Crossroads: An Insider's Look at the Past, Present, and Future of Contemporary Christian Music* (Nashville: Broadman and Holman, 1998).

29. Wagner suggests the first wave was the pentecostal movement of the early 1900s, the second wave was the charismatic movement of the mid 1960s, and now the third has just ensued, and we are still within its wake. See C. Peter Wagner, *The Third Wave of the Holy Spirit: Encountering the Power of Signs and Wonders Today,* foreword by John Wimber (Ann Arbor, Mich.: Servant, 1988).

30. John Wimber had initial ties with Calvary Chapel and later developed significant ties to the church growth movement. In the mid 1970s, C. Peter Wagner invited Wimber to be a partner in establishing the Charles E. Fuller Institute of Evangelism and Church Growth at Fuller Theological Seminary.

alone) pay a yearly fee and, according to the honor system, file reports of CCLI song use.[31]

Today, these major publishing houses — Maranatha! Music, Vineyard Music Group, and Integrity Music — are generating more than just worship music. In 1992, Maranatha! Music combined resources with CCM Publications to produce *Worship Leader* magazine, the "mouthpiece of the [Contemporary Worship] movement," as its editor, Chuck Fromm, calls it. Soon after, Maranatha! Music started hosting worship leader workshops multiple times a year, tough acts that VMG and Integrity Music have gladly followed. Only recently, Integrity Music has teamed up with both Liberty University and Regent University to offer degree programs in worship studies.[32]

> *"The arts of worship are created not merely for the sake of beauty and in freedom from human and institutional expectation. They are created for the sake of God's people in order to open hearts as well as minds; to touch people deeply, strengthen their faith, and evoke a transformation in their lives."*
>
> Clayton J. Schmit, *Too Deep for Words* (Louisville: Westminster John Knox, 2002), p. 25

While Calvary Chapel and Vineyard Christian Fellowship had drawn church leaders' attention to the West Coast, Willow Creek Community Church soon drew their attention to the heartland. Essentially born from a high school rock band that covered the tunes of Larry Norman, Michael Omartian, and Chuck Girard (all associated with Calvary Chapel), Willow Creek became an incorporated church community in 1975.[33] Designed to reach the nonreligious, Willow Creek services have always included drama, multimedia, and contemporary music.[34] For nearly fifteen years Willow Creek's exponential growth went without notice; then, in 1989, the media turned this mega-church into a mega-spectacle. *Time* came, and NBC's *Today*

---

31. Christian Copyright Licensing, Inc., http://www.ccli.com (1 August 2003).

32. Robb Redman, "Expanding Your Worship Worldview: Education and Training for Worship Leaders," *Worship Leader* 9, no. 3 (May/June 2000): 18-20, 22.

33. Hybels and Hybels, *Rediscovering Church*, pp. 27ff.

34. Bill Hybels suggests Willow Creek's "approach isn't very different from what Billy Graham has done with nearly universal blessing for the last several decades" (*Rediscovering Church*, p. 174).

History Takes a Hit

Lester Ruth

Are there historic precedents for introducing popular idioms of music into worship to make it a tool for evangelism? Some proponents of "contemporary" worship music would lead us to believe that this was the case with some of the greatest Protestant leaders. Frequently, for example, these proponents cite Martin Luther and the Methodist Wesley brothers (John and Charles) as examples of those who intentionally adopted popular musical forms to reach the unchurched.

This portrayal is very poor history. It is not the whole story. For one thing, it is a gross simplification of where these men actually got their tunes. More accurate histories point out that they used music from a variety of sources. A recent study of the 148 tunes found in John Wesley's published tune books shows how Wesley included tunes from German chorales, from metrical psalters previously published in English, from then-contemporary composers influenced by the Baroque style of music, and from other English tune books, among other sources. Likewise, Luther not only adapted secular folk songs but also borrowed tunes from Gregorian chant and medieval hymns. Indeed, Luther continued to advocate the use of Latin in church music in certain instances as well as complex multivoice music by choirs. This actual variety does not square with modern proponents who use these men as examples of reducing worship music to one style for evangelistic purposes.

Even "bar" tunes have likely been misunderstood. As one scholar has pointed out, this piece of the story about Luther results from a misunderstanding of technical German musical terminology.

Show, and even *Fortune* magazine, which gave it significant coverage in a five-page spread entitled, "Turning Around the Lord's Business."[35] While the media's take on their ministry was not always welcomed by the Willow Creek staff,[36] it certainly heightened interest in the Willow Creek way. Hence the formation in 1992 of the Willow Creek Association, which today serves more than 7,200 member churches around the world with conferences, consultations, worship resources, and subscriptions to *WCA News, Willow Creek Monthly,* and Lee Strobel's *Defining Moments* Leadership Tape Series.

35. Barbara Dolan, "Full House at Willow Creek," *Time* 133, no. 10 (6 March 1989): 60. Thomas A. Steward, "Turning around the Lord's Business," *Fortune* 120, no. 7 (25 September 1989): 116-17.

36. Hybels and Hybels, *Rediscovering Church,* p. 103.

"Bar" does not refer to a place of entertainment but to a kind of phrase structure in music.

This common portrayal of Luther and the Wesleys is also poor history because it misses the way these men really understood worship and the role of music within it. For one thing, it is not fair to place modern "tactical" ideas about using worship primarily as a strategy or tool for evangelism in the minds of these historical figures. For them worship was not just a way to reach the unchurched but was the activity of the church itself. Music should be appropriate, not just to reach outsiders, but to fulfill certain worship purposes, particularly the participation of the people. Luther, in particular, was sensitive about worship changes lest they disenfranchise some already in church.

By focusing on the style of music, modern proponents also underplay the content of these histori-cal figures' hymns. Wesley, for example, considered Methodist hymns to be a body of sung theology. They had theological breadth and richness. Look closely at modern advocates of "popular" styles of music for worship. Are they as concerned about the theological content of worship music as were the historical figures whom they cite?

Finally, this is poor history because it misses a fuller use of these men as great evangelists and agents of renewal. Just adopting contemporary music lets us off the hook too easily in what it means to follow their example. Why isolate their work in music? Why not emphasize just as much their work in restoring the Lord's Supper as the lifeblood of the gospel in the church's activity, including its evangelism?

There are many good reasons to use contemporary worship music. Inaccurate history should not be one of them.

In recent years, the music of Contemporary Worship has continued to diversify. In the mid 1990s Hillsongs Music, featuring Darlene Zschech, and the Brooklyn Tabernacle Choir, under the leadership of Carol Cymbala, began presenting new possibilities for choral ensembles in Contemporary Worship. Their CDs have topped the Christian music charts, and their sheet music is being back-ordered.

At the same time, the music of Generation X has found its own postmodern niche within Contemporary Worship. From edgy industrial drum loops to melancholic ballads, the musical temperaments of alternative rock are being brought to the fore by performers such as Matt Redman, Delirious?, and Sonic Flood. Major publishing houses have created their own spin-off labels for the "raw emotion" of "music for the new generation," labels such as Maranatha!'s "Alternative Praise" and Integrity's "Vertical Music."

Worshiping communities that have tuned their dial to postmodernity incorporate not only an eclectic range of music but also art and incense, dance and candles, in order to attach all five senses to the experience of worshiping God. "Being creative," says Mark Driscoll of Mars Hill Fellowship, Seattle, "is tough work, but we believe art is that region between heaven and earth that connects the two. To experience God is often the highest form of knowing, and the entire worship experience must be more than presentation *about* God."[37] To enhance the experience, especially for a postmodern crowd to whom "pastiche is king," worship bands at Mars Hill will lead a reworked Scottish folk tune in one moment and, in the next, an originally composed rock song, with the edgy sung-speech and distorted guitar of grunge bands like Nirvana.[38]

In order to keep up with these changing interests in worship, or with the size of their congregation—or just to keep up—some churches have undertaken the "video venue" model. Among the first was North Coast Church in Vista, California. Taking their cue from shopping malls and movie theatres, leaders at North Coast now give their Saturday evening and Sunday morning worshipers choices. Several services take place on the same campus at the same time, but all are synchronized so that each receives the same "live" sermon via video feed. *North Coast Live* meets in the main auditorium led by a full worship team and featuring the "live" teaching. *Traditions* offers coffee and pastries, "intimate and nostalgic" worship, and then the teaching onscreen. In the *Video Café* worshipers may sip a Starbucks and relax in a coffee klatsch atmosphere that features an acoustic band and, again, the message onscreen. At *The Edge*, where a plugged-in band produces high energy worship with a cutting

37. Quoted in Sally Morgenthaler, "Out of the Box: Authentic Worship in a Post-Modern Culture," *Worship Leader* 7, no. 3 (May-June 1998): 25.
38. MP3 Real Audio files of Mars Hill bands are available at http://www.marshill.fm/worship/music.htm (12 July 2002).

edge sound, Starbucks coffee and Mountain Dew are "a necessity . . . in order to keep up with the worship."[39] Here, too, an onscreen sermon follows.

More recently, video feed technology has provided a means for churches to plant satellite congregations. In March 2002, Willow Creek launched its first "regional ministry" in Wheaton, Illinois. For weekend and mid-week services, live worship complements a videocast of the teaching that takes place at the South Barrington site. For Willow Creek, the goal is "to become a multisite campus, to be one church in many locations."[40]

Clearly a historical account as sketchy as this cannot say it all (we haven't even broached the experimentalism of "alternative worship,"[41] nor the emergence of "home church"[42]), but it says enough to show that Contemporary Worship is a complex, multifaceted phenomenon that has burgeoned in North American Christian culture for at least the last half century. If we look a little further back in religious history, however, we discover that "contemporary worship" is, in fact, something of a recurring phenomenon in the Christian church. For example, if we trace the roots of the gospel hymns that gave early rise to the Southern gospel and black gospel music of the 1900s, we quickly uncover a connection to the North American revivals of the Second Great Awakening of the 1800s, which were related to John Wesley's influence in England and North America in the 1700s, which was anticipated by the Pietist Movement on the European

> "[A] worship leader from a Vineyard in Chicago told us that southern California Vineyard music is just too mellow for their taste, so they rearrange it with a stronger beat and a more urban, 'bluesy' flavor."
>
> Donald E. Miller, *Reinventing American Protestantism* (Berkeley: University of California Press, 1997), p. 84

39. North Coast Church, "The Edge: Happenings at the Edge," http://www .northcoastchurch.com/theedge/happenings.htm (1 August 2003).

40. Willow Creek Community Church, "Regional Upate," http://www.willowcreek.org/ regional_update.asp and http://www.willowcreek.org/chapter2/regional.asp (1 August 2003).

41. See http://www.alternativeworship.org/ (1 August 2003).

42. See "Home Church" at http://www.home-church.org; and "House Church Central" at http://www.hccentral.com (1 August 2003).

**Contemporary Worship,
Contemporary Language?**

Margo G. Houts

I

It is December and the choir is rehearsing hymns, carols, and praise songs for its four Christmas Eve services. Chloe Davis observes that the Director of Music has replaced some of the inclusive language in the hymnal (e.g., "all," "we," "humankind") with more traditional language (e.g., "man," "men").

"Why not sing the inclusive version already printed in our hymnals?" she asks, puzzled.

The Director explains, "We want to help those who grew up hearing and memorizing traditional wording to worship so that they're not jolted by unfamiliar substitutions."

"Yes," Chloe nods in understanding, "but what about those who, like me, are distracted from worship by 'man' and 'men'? And what about those who did not grow up hearing church music, who will feel left out, as I do, by all these 'he's' and 'him's'?"

II

It is Easter, and the Family Ministries intern invites the children to join her at the chancel steps. Excitedly, they peer into a basket filled with brightly colored eggs. Each egg represents one aspect of the Passion story, and their role is to name the meaning of each color. "The green egg? That's right, green like the palm branches that greet Jesus as he enters Jerusalem. The red-colored egg? That's right, wine that Jesus pours during the Last Supper. White? You got it! That's the bread that he shares with the disciples." So far so good. Then the intern holds up a black-colored egg. A child's hand shoots up, his voice confident: "Black is for Judas, the traitor!" It was not the answer the intern was looking for, but not wanting to stop the momentum, she echoes the child's answer, "black is for treachery," and quickly moves on to the next colored egg. On the chancel steps, in a sea of Euro-American faces, two African-American children see and hear all.

---

continent as early as the 1600s. During the 1600s, Pietists responded to what they took to be the church's dead orthodoxy and cold spirituality. Those who advocated reform urged leaders of the church to move people's hearts rather than stuff their heads, in order to stir a true Christian faith marked by a fervid pursuit of godliness.[43] This was something of John Wesley's theme, which was adopted and warmed with an evangelistic zeal by Francis Asbury on the western

43. This is a significant theme in Philipp Jakob Spener's *Pia Desideria*, 1675. Early in his treatise, Spener makes this point after citing several fathers of the early church.

III

Whenever I have the opportunity to teach, I invite my students to complete a survey. Along with questions about why they are taking my course, and what occupies their leisure time, the survey includes questions about inclusive language: Are you familiar with it, and do you use it? What about your home congregation?

Year after year, these surveys indicate that the majority of my students, and most of their congregations (whether mainline or nondenominational, Euro-American or multicultural), remain either largely unaware of or minimally concerned about inclusive language. This is true not just with respect to language for God, but also the less controversial topic of language for human beings. It simply is not a pressing issue.

Often, churches embracing more contemporary forms of worship (nonliturgical format, praise songs, praise teams, guitars and drums) have retained traditional forms of language. For example, *Come Celebrate: Music for Contemporary Worship*

(Abingdon, 1999) includes an assortment of standard hymns whose tempo and style have been radically modernized, yet whose traditional androcentric wording has been retained (e.g., "men" instead of "people.") Those for whom language *is* an issue – especially mainline and liberationist seminary professors and denominational staff – have had minimal involvement in, and consequently minimal impact upon, the Contemporary Worship scene. The ironic result is that "contemporary" worship often reflects "traditional" language, while more "contemporary language" flourishes mostly in "traditional" worship.

∼

Talking Points:

• What do you suppose fuels this irony?

• In her book *In Her Own Rite: Constructing Feminist Liturgical Tradition* (Abingdon, 1990), Marjorie Procter-Smith differentiates and evaluates three approaches for transforming one's language,

continued . . .

---

shore of the Atlantic. Within decades, the Second Great Awakening had been fully fledged, and Charles Grandison Finney was advocating the use of "new measures" in worship so that the church might "succeed in gaining the attention of the world to religion."[44]

These themes sound a familiar tune. Given the synopsis above, it seems almost inevitable that history would give us the genre of worship we know today as Contemporary Worship.

44. Charles Grandison Finney, *Lectures on Revivals of Religion,* ed. William G. McLoughlin (Cambridge, Mass.: Harvard University Press, 1960), p. 272.

or that of a community: using nonsexist, inclusive, and emancipatory language. She writes: "Nonsexist language seeks to avoid gender-specific terms. Inclusive language seeks to balance gender references. Emancipatory language seeks to transform language use and to challenge stereotypical gender references" (p. 36, emphasis added).

While nonsexist and inclusive approaches each have their strengths and weaknesses, Procter-Smith elevates emancipatory language as the more productive goal. Emancipatory language extends well beyond gender, for it also challenges how the community of faith thinks about race, class, age, ability, and other (often hidden) privileges in light of the gospel. It is language — not only verbal, but visual and physical as well — that calls forth change:

language that makes visible not just personal piety but corporate and communal dimensions of faith; language that underscores the costs of discipleship at least as much as the rewards; language that juxtaposes the vertical dimension of worship with the horizontal dimension, recognizing that one may not authentically relate to and love God without relating to and loving others (Matt. 25:31-46; 1 John 4:7-12).

How might Procter-Smith evaluate each of the two scenarios above?

• In what ways might some, whether members or guests, feel left out in your church? How can our language be a way of expressing hospitality in worship? What are some approaches you might use to transform this situation, and what guidelines for language would you like to see applied?

But just what *is* Contemporary Worship?

Rather than attempting a definition that would require inevitable qualification, let's explore Contemporary Worship's characteristic features (only a few of which might be necessary for a church to call its worship "Contemporary"), allowing them to instruct us as we go.

Features of Contemporary Worship

It's clear, for instance, that churches that are into Contemporary Worship are into contemporary culture; that is, many want to bring contemporary culture into their contemporary worship, and for that they install all of culture's technological accoutrements. While ministers continue to augment their sermons with colorful narratives and drama troupe performances, JumboTron screens and video projection units now allow preachers to illustrate their sermons with clips from movies, prime-time TV, or the news. Using PowerPoint®, churches not only enable congregational singing with projected texts but also enhance their worship spaces with savvy graphics and illustrate their announcements with digital photos. Whether as part of a church's original design or in a church retrofit for this purpose, catwalks and masts are installed to fly theatrical stage lights and state-of-the-art speaker clusters.

Contemporary culture affects not just what worshipers see in church, but especially what they hear. Once upon a time, worship was led primarily by a minister and an organist, who might employ the help of a cantor or choir. Today, Contemporary Worship is led by an ensemble of lay people, often referred to as the "worship team" or "praise band." A drummer, pianist, guitarist, and any number of vocalists are common to nearly all such ensembles, while, given a church's resources, instrumentalists of any stripe might be invited to join them.

Typically this ensemble is responsible for presenting all of a church's service music, each element of which might be cast into either of two general categories: that which is performed simply for the people's listening and that which is performed to lead the people's singing. For people's listening, accomplished bands play tunes from just about any genre — Christian rock, classic rock, rhythm and blues, jazz, folk, gospel, reggae, or ska. In the interest of making the sounds of worship as familiar as the sounds of a favorite radio station, church bands usher these genres into worship, vamping original tunes or revamping old ones, like "Crown Him with Many Crowns" or "O For a Thousand Tongues to Sing."

While this range of musical genres is not excluded from the repertoire of songs that a band plays to lead people's singing, one can expect to find here a significant number of the Scripture songs and praise choruses that have been published in the last three decades specifically for Contemporary Worship. Simple harmonies, easy melodies, and repeated lyrics are all penned for their accessibility. Lyricists frequently lift their texts from Scripture, and when they don't, they write poetry using the conversational, even colloquial, religious parlance of evangelical America today.

Worship leaders, or "emcees" as they are referred to in some venues, employ this same rhetoric in the spoken transitions and prayers that move worship along. Those who plan Contemporary Worship strive for a seamless event. They strive to keep the service moving, to keep the pace up and the "dead time" down. To attain this seamless effect, spoken transitions and prayers — usually short and few — are often padded with an instrumental riff and they're planned to sound "unplanned."

This choreographed spontaneity translates into a kind of ceremonial minimalism in Contemporary Worship, and it's manifested in several ways. We've already noted one — the colloquial language with which worship is led. Accordingly, worship leaders refrain from using biblical-theological terms, such as "sin" and "grace," and instead give these concepts narrative expression like "turning a wrong corner," and "getting an undeserved favor." Moreover, because sacraments are rich with theological meaning and mystery and would likely be unintelligible to the uninitiated, churches rarely administer them in the nonbeliever's, or seeker's, service, and instead reserve them for after that service or for a believer's service. For this reason, baptismal fonts and communion tables, even pulpits and crosses, are often absent in spaces newly designed for Contemporary Worship. Sanctuaries look less

> *"Many ministers include in their sermons a joke or two which may or may not be relevant to what the sermons are about but in any case are supposed to warm up the congregation and demonstrate that preachers are just plain folks like everybody else.*
>
> *"There are two dangers in this. One is that if the joke is a good one, the chances are it will be the only part of the sermon that anybody remembers on Monday morning. The other is that when preachers tell jokes, it is often an unconscious way of telling both their congregations and themselves that the Gospel is all very well but in the last analysis not to be taken too seriously."*
>
> Frederick Buechner, *Wishful Thinking: A Seeker's ABC* (San Francisco: HarperSanFrancisco, 1993), p. 57

like a "church" and more like a concert stage or a convention hall, a club or a living room.[45] Ministers once received reverential titles and dressed in robes as symbols of their calling; but today in Contemporary Worship, ministers are encouraged to put off whatever might be mistaken as a put-on. So first names and business casual have replaced these titles and dress, even what we once called "Sunday best," as ministers and worship leaders try to fit themselves into an informal atmosphere and make themselves more approachable. Churches rarely print liturgies or purchase prayer books for Contemporary Worship. Instead, worshipers follow a projected order of service, often with the general expectation that vigorous songs of praise will lead to contemplative songs of worship, followed by a message and a final song of praise. Rarely will worship planners include responsive readings, prayers of confession, or words of benediction.

So what's the point of minimizing ceremonious features of worship? It seems the purposes may be sifted to two, namely, to make worship accessible and to make it authentic. Certainly neither of these is exclusive of the other, but, then, either might take a sort of precedence over the other depending on a church's motive for undertaking Contemporary Worship. Exploring these motives and their relative emphases on accessibility and authenticity leads one to see that Contemporary Worship — again, capital C, capital W — is really a genus of which there are a few species, and that these species have been crossbreeding.

45. See Tim Stafford, "God Is in the Blueprints," *Christianity Today* 42, no. 10 (7 September 1998): 76-82, for explorations of these first two descriptions. Then, for the second two, consider the description of Solomon's Porch at the outset of this chapter, or surf the Web to find worshiping communities like Graceland at Santa Cruz Bible Church, Santa Cruz, California, which sets up round tables and chairs in the seating area of its worship space in order to create the lively club atmosphere so appealing to the Gen X crowd there (www.santacruzbible.org/graceland, 12 July 2002).

REASONS FOR UNDERTAKING CONTEMPORARY WORSHIP

A multitude of churches throughout North America have undertaken Contemporary Worship for the sake of evangelism. We've already noted two big ones, Willow Creek and Ginghamsburg; but there are others, including Community Church of Joy, Phoenix, Arizona, and Saddleback Community Church, Lake Forest, California. While each qualifies as a mega-church, only one, Willow Creek, is decidedly "adenominational."[46] The others are United Methodist, Evangelical Lutheran, and Southern Baptist respectively, which indicates that this evangelistic motive isn't denominationally — or even "adenominationally" — isolated. And there are, of course, literally thousands of churches of every size and kind thriving in their shadows. One might say that these North American mega-churches are like the old English cathedrals, which served as liturgical laboratories that set the tone for outlying parishes.[47]

Leaders in these contemporary North American "laboratories" advocate planning worship for the unchurched, the nonbeliever, the "pre-Christian." Read their literature, listen to their tapes, attend their conferences, or visit their Websites: there you find a longing to make the gospel accessible to the nonreligious by making worship accessible. The idea is that if the gospel is going to be accessible, then it must be introduced through a personally relevant topic in a culturally relevant setting.

To strike the hearts of nonbelievers, churches, they suggest, should address in worship the "felt needs" of their target congregation. On Wednesday mornings at Ginghamsburg Church, this is precisely where worship planning begins. Upon hearing lead pastor Mike Slaughter's "word" for the week, the planning team works with the idea to "identify the felt need that connects with the seek-

46. Michael Maudlin and Edward Gilbreath, "Selling Out the House of God?" *Christianity Today* 38, no. 8 (8 July 1994): 25.

47. John Witvliet, "The Blessing and Bane of the North American Mega-Church: Implications for Twenty-first Century Congregational Song," *Jahrbuch für Liturgik und Hymnologie* 37 (1998): 201.

er."[48] As planning progresses, questions persist: Is this practical? Is it relevant? Has the felt need been met? And, most important to the team members, So what? How is all of this going to be interpreted by somebody who's never been in church before?[49] Rick Warren of Saddleback Church and Timothy Wright of Community Church of Joy express much the same view, and they do so with enthusiasm.[50] Bill Hybels, on the other hand, offers a word of caution, urging ministers to resist the temptation to develop a "junk food preaching diet" that fails to reflect Scripture as a whole and ultimately thwarts spiritual growth.[51]

Still, all of them agree it's futile to deliver a personally relevant message in a culturally irrelevant setting. Worship must be accessible, and for that, say those who plan Contemporary Worship for the sake of evangelism, churches should usher out traditional elements and usher in contemporary media, pretty much along the lines we've explored. Together, these are the means of making worship "safe" for the irreligious;[52] these are the means of removing cultural barriers for the uninitiated.[53]

But different people have different barriers, and even different "needs." So, as noted before, there's an ongoing propagation of churches and services that appeal to, say, specific generational profiles: this one for Boomers, this one for Busters, this one for Xers. Sights and sounds and sets may change, but the hope is the same — that the arts of contemporary culture will be effectively "harnessed" for a dynamic evangelistic ministry.[54] In churches that undertake Contemporary Worship for the purpose of evangelism, there is an

48. Slaughter, *Out on the Edge*, p. 78.
49. Slaughter et al., CD Rom "Multi-Sensory Worship," with *Out on the Edge*.
50. Rick Warren, *The Purpose-Driven Church* (Grand Rapids: Zondervan, 1995), p. 295; Timothy Wright, *A Community of Joy: How to Create Contemporary Worship* (Nashville: Abingdon, 1994), p. 86.
51. Hybels and Hybels, *Rediscovering Church*, p. 185.
52. Rick Warren, *The Purpose-Driven Church*, p. 251; see also Hybels and Hybels, *Rediscovering Church*, p. 206.
53. Walt Kallestad of Community Church of Joy, in *Entertainment Evangelism*, p. 69.
54. Hybels and Hybels, *Rediscovering Church*, p. 174.

underlying sense that worship is authenticated by the measure of its accessibility, by the degree to which it delivers God's answers to people's felt needs. As Mike Slaughter puts it, "Worship happens when the presence of God is bridged with people's felt needs in their life context." If that hasn't happened, worship hasn't happened.[55]

But there are other leaders of Contemporary Worship who might say simply, "Worship happens when the presence of God is bridged." To them, worship is a bridge between us and God, and the idea of crafting a service to address a seeker is unsavory. Instead, a service should be crafted to address God, to generate an encounter with the living God through fervent worship, or "ascription of worth" to God.[56] Such worship, says Sally Morgenthaler, will be evangelistic, because while revealing God, it reveals good news. This might be "evangelism by accident," she admits,[57] but what people yearn for today is God — an "experiencing-is-believing" encounter with God. So if the church hopes to have any "impact on our culture," then "worship is going to need to feature direct, supernatural interaction with God."[58]

Although fresh, what Morgenthaler here presents is actually a variation on a theme. That is to say, Morgenthaler's ideas about worship arise from themes that Judson Cornwall, Jack Hayford, Bob Sorge, Ron Kenoly, and LaMar Boschman have been sounding for several years, contrasting "God's simple route of approach" with the church's "complex rites of religion."[59] Hayford, for example, worries about the "historic approach to the doctrine of worship," where "the intellectual and artistic demands of religious duty may easily intrude upon the best intent of the worshiper, and suddenly we become those 'who draw near with their lips but their heart is far from me.'"[60]

55. Slaughter, *Out on the Edge*, p. 73.
56. Sally Morgenthaler, *Worship Evangelism: Inviting Believers into the Presence of God* (Grand Rapids: Zondervan, 1995), pp. 46f.
57. Morgenthaler, *Worship Evangelism*, p. 40.
58. Morgenthaler, *Worship Evangelism*, p. 66.
59. Bob Sorge, *Let Us Draw Near* (South Plainfield, N.J.: Bridge Publishing, 1977), p. 165.
60. Jack W. Hayford, *Worship His Majesty* (Waco, Tex.: Word Books, 1987), p. 22.

And what is this "simple route of approach"? "Praise and worship," which has found a home not only in charismatic communities, where it first was born, but also in seeker-targeted ministries, where it has since been adopted. In an interview with *Christianity Today,* Bill Hybels once referred to what takes place in his auditorium on Sunday mornings as "Spirit-anointed drama, multi-media, and contemporary Christian music."[61] Or consider, for example, Saddleback's rubric for worship planning, an acronym, I.M.P.A.C.T.: Those who gather must be *Inspired* to enter God's presence with fast-paced musical *Movement* that kindles their hearts and hands; *Praise* (upbeat songs about God) should subside to *Adoration* (slow songs addressed to God), so that worshipers might yield in *Commitment;* after the message, one song will *Tie It All Together.*[62]

Conclusion

Any given Sunday, worship takes shape in a variety of ways, in a variety of communities, for a variety of reasons. Thousands gather in churches made "safe" for nonbelievers. Thousands more gather in churches where worship leaders strive to "make God known" through a progression of songs that lead one "into the very presence of God." In some churches, worshipers participate in the weekly recitation of creeds and celebration of sacraments. In others, they worship "in tongues," singing the psalms, hymns, and spiritual songs of brothers and sisters in Christ from around the world and right next-door.

To many readers, this discussion of worship might seem old hat. They've found their "niche" in worship, and so have those with whom they disagreed ten or twenty years ago. But some com-

61. Quoted in Maudlin and Gilbreath, "Selling Out the House of God?" p. 23.
62. Warren, *Purpose-Driven Church,* p. 256; or Purpose Driven, "Saddleback's Frequently Asked Questions: Magnification/Music," © 1998-2001 Purpose Driven, http://www. purpose-driven.com/pdc/faqs/music_faq.html (30 April 2001). Compare this to Barry Leisch, *The New Worship* (Grand Rapids: Baker, 1996), and Bob Sorge, *Exploring Worship* (Canandaigua, N.Y.: Bob Sorge © 1987).

munities are still conflicted, which means the body of Christ is still discomfited. Throughout the church, in communities of every persuasion, ministers, worship leaders, and worshipers are beginning to wonder, Now what? What's next? Their enthusiasm for authentic worship persists, but now that contemporary worship (not just Contemporary Worship) has ripened, they're asking new questions about the influence of culture, the nature of church, and the essence of worship. Such questions run deep in the history of the Christian church, and today they're being asked anew.

Chapter 3

At the Intersection
of Church and World

TOP-TEN LISTS. A BLACK GOSPEL GROOVE. Batik vestments. A mariachi band.

If these details from our previous chapter illustrate anything about present-day worship, they illustrate at least this: that believers throughout the world are striving to embody Christian worship in ways that reflect their local setting, that connect to their culture. In North America, especially among the leaders of Contemporary Worship, this means striving to connect with contemporary *popular* culture. For example:

• *In some churches, major sporting events, such as the Super Bowl, become a super segue for the gospel. Viewers gather to watch the game, shown on the JumboTron screens in the sanctuary; then the half-time show is pre-empted by a minister's introduction to the gospel and an invitation to respond.*

• *Just before reading the Scripture text for his sermon, a minister removes his sport coat, loosens his tie, and rolls up his sleeves. Throughout the sermon he wanders up and down the aisles, one hand resting in the pocket of his khakis, the other gesturing to emphasize his points.*

- *A worship band leads the seventeenth-century hymn "Praise to the Lord, the Almighty" with a few vocalists and a percussive tom-drum riff that suggests an explosive, almost tribal, dance.*

- *Midway through her sermon, a minister stops her monologue to show a clip from Spike Lee's film 4* Little Girls, *a documentary about the 1963 bombing of a black Baptist church in Birmingham, Alabama.*

- *The Lord's Table is prepared with grape juice and goldfish crackers.*

- *A service of confession includes the singing of Frank Sinatra's "My Way," its final refrain voiced over with a prayer: Lord, we do try to live life on our terms instead of yours. Then the congregation responds, singing "Great Is Thy Faithfulness," or "People Who Need People Are the Luckiest People in the World."*[1]

No doubt such connections to contemporary popular culture will elicit a variety of responses. Some readers might whip out a pencil: a check marked here and a name scrawled there will remind them of their hopes for a future worship planning session. Others might puzzle over two or three of these scenarios and gape in disbelief at another one or two. Some might find a couple of these sketches sacrilegious. Put these folk together for a discussion and their opposing convictions are sure to rub against each other, generating a good deal of heat.

So what causes the friction? What, at bottom, divides our judgments?

What's controversial about Contemporary Worship, even among some who consider themselves its enthusiasts, is that in its attempt to be relevant to contemporary culture, Contemporary Worship employs cultural forms that might clash with the gospel, or with a reverent attitude toward God, or with a respectful approach to God's people. If we worship God in a rock idiom, can we forget that rock music in popular culture has been mostly "into" drugs, sex, and rebellion against God,

---

1. Tex Sample, *The Spectacle of Worship in a Wired World* (Nashville: Abingdon, 1998), p. 115.

The Greatest Drama Ever Staged

Dorothy Sayers

Official Christianity, of late years, has been having what is known as "a bad press." We are constantly assured that the churches are empty because preachers insist too much upon doctrine — "dull dogma," as people call it. The fact is the precise opposite. It is the neglect of dogma that makes for dullness. The Christian faith is the most exciting drama that ever staggered the imagination of man — and the dogma is the drama. . . .

Possibly we might prefer not to take this tale too seriously — there are disquieting points about it. Here we had a man of Divine character walking and talking among us — and what did we find to do with Him? The common people, indeed, "heard Him gladly"; but our leading authorities in Church and State considered that He talked too much and uttered too many disquieting truths. So we bribed one of His friends to hand Him over quietly to the police, and we tried Him on a rather vague charge of creating a disturbance, and had Him publicly flogged and hanged on the common gallows, "thanking God we were rid of a knave." All this was not very creditable to us, even if He was (as many people thought and think) only a harmless crazy preacher. But if the Church is right about Him, it was more discreditable still; for the man we hanged was God Almighty.

So that is the outline of the official story — the tale of the time when God was the under-dog and got beaten, when He submitted to the conditions He had laid down and became a man like the men He had made, and the men He had made broke Him and killed Him. This is the dogma we find so dull — this terrifying drama of which God is the victim and hero.

If this is dull, then what, in Heaven's name, is worthy to be called exciting?

Excerpt from "The Greatest Drama Ever Staged *Is the Official Creed of Christendom*," in *Creed or Chaos? and Other Essays in Popular Theology* (London: Methuen and Co., 1947), pp. 1, 3.

---

and that worship isn't?[2] Does it matter that some cultural events, such as the Super Bowl, inspire gambling and consumerism, and so stand in stark contrast with mainstream readings of Scripture?

On the one hand, the values of the Christian faith and the anti-values of certain forms of popular entertainment seem to run in opposite directions. This, as *Newsweek* says in a cover story on Christian entertainment, is the elephant in the middle of the Christian rock band.[3] On

2. Calvin Stapert, in *Chimes* (Grand Rapids: Calvin College), 5 October 1979, p. 7; also Michael Linton's book review in *First Things*, no. 100 (February 2000): 63-64.

3. Lorraine Ali, "The Glorious Rise of Christian Pop," *Newsweek* 138, no. 3 (16 July 2001): 43.

the other hand, if worship fails to engage with the way people live their lives today, churches risk losing some who would be believers and perhaps others who already are. People might not connect with God or with the gospel, especially if popular culture is their "native language."

The dilemma is not simple, given that it's often hard to gauge "the way people live their lives today." For instance, would we think of medieval plainchant as "nonpopular"? Then how do we explain the rave reviews[4] and record-breaking CD sales of *Chant*, sung by the Benedictine Monks of Santo Domingo de Silos? Or what about sixteenth-century polyphony and responsorial prayers — would we consider these to be "alien" today? Then how do we explain Sunday compline at St. Mark's Episcopal in Seattle, Washington, for which hundreds of twenty-somethings gather each week, just as they have for decades?[5]

> *"When religion presses back against the dominant culture, both are changed as a result of the encounter."*
>
> Stephen Carter, *God's Name in Vain* (New York: Basic, 2000), p. 172

In the middle of such complex situations, we face a fundamental challenge. How do we translate or embody or "inculturate" our worship of God in cultural forms that will reach our neighbors but will not distort the gospel? Answers to this question, manifested in worship practices like those explored at the outset of this chapter, are hotly debated in the church today, and the arguments matter. We're not talking here about mere differences in taste (*de gustibus non disputandum est*,[6] as the saying goes), but about judgments of fittingness. We're wrestling with questions of integrity: are we upholding the integrity of the gospel and of Christian worship even as we translate them into fresh cultural idioms?

Translation, of course, is always hazardous. Every translation is itself an interpretation. As a result, a translation opens hearers not only

---

4. For instance a *Rolling Stone* reviewer (no. 684, 16 June 1994, p. 106) says this music is "some of the most purely entrancing sound ever composed . . . from the heart, unselfconscious, nakedly direct." See also a review in *Spin*, December 1994.

5. Lynn Neary, "Generation X Spirituality in Seattle," *All Things Considered*, National Public Radio, 1 March 1999.

6. "With respect to tastes there can be no debate."

to the possibility of new understandings but also to the possibility of new misunderstandings. So when we translate, how do we know we are saying the *same* thing with different words? How do we know we haven't said a *different* thing with those different words? Then, too, every message is affected by its medium. This is notoriously true of poetry and prose, even when they're translated just into the words of a different language. Such difficulties deepen when poetry and prose — or psalmody and parable, song and sacrament — are "translated" into the multimedia of a particular culture. And so our central question returns: Once the gospel has been translated (perhaps into a rock idiom), do we still have the gospel according to Jesus Christ, or have we fashioned a gospel according to contemporary culture? And how do we know?

Answering such questions requires sound judgment. At bottom, these issues raise the hard questions of what it means to be "resident aliens," as Stanley Hauerwas and William Willimon once put it;[7] to be *in* the world but not *of* the world, as the apostle John first put it.

These are exactly the questions we mean to raise in this chapter, largely because the center of debate over Contemporary Worship lies within their range. Here we will say that cultural translation is inevitable, that it's desirable, but that it's also risky. Here we will discover that whether we're this side of the fence, that side of the fence, or *on* the fence, we all need the gift of discernment. We need spiritual discernment to judge not a difference in taste, because taste is too weak a criterion for the debate, and not a difference in biblical prescription, because that's too strong. No, we need spiritual discernment to judge what's *fitting* for Christian worship.

DEFINING CULTURE

First a word about culture. As with Contemporary Worship, culture is a phenomenon that defies concise definition. It's the sort of term

7. Stanley Hauerwas and William Willimon, *Resident Aliens: Life in the Christian Colony* (Nashville: Abingdon, 1989).

Testing Christian Taste: Twelve Assumptions

Frank Burch Brown

Let me . . . [set] forth twelve assumptions that I hope could fruitfully guide discussions of aesthetic taste as they arise in the next stage of religious, and specifically Christian, development in relation to the arts. . . . I regard them as assumptions or premises rather than as goals; but one could also look on them as habits of mind useful for exercising Christian taste in healthy ways. . . .

1. There are many kinds of good taste, and many kinds of good religious art and music. In view of cultural diversity, it would be extremely odd if that were not true.

2. Not all kinds of good art and music are equally good for worship, let alone for every tradition or faith community. In terms of worship, therefore, it is not enough that a work or style of art be likeable; it must also be appropriate.

3. There are various appropriately Christian modes of mediating religious experience artistically – from radically transcendent to radically immanent in a sense of the sacred; from exuberantly abundant to starkly minimal in means; from prophetic to pastoral in tone; from instructive to meditative in aim.

4. Every era and cultural context tends to develop new forms of sacred music and art, which to begin with often seem secular to many people.

5. Because every musical/aesthetic style calls for a particular kind of attunement, no one person can

---

we employ with the assumption that whatever our mind associates with it will approximate whatever our listener's mind associates with it, when in fact that might not be the case. In general conversations, the term is often used so broadly it loses its point. It makes culture out to be monolithic and static — which it never is. We'll need instead a focused description of culture that suits culture's complexities.

In one of his essays, Gordon Lathrop, citing the study of two twentieth-century anthropologists, notes that there appear to be no fewer than 164 general definitions of culture scattered about, each bearing its own nuance.[8] We'd be foolish to uproot that many definitions, attempting to cross them for some kind of consummate hybrid. Still, it's valuable to explore a few definitions for the sake of a common understanding in our discussion.

8. Gordon Lathrop, "Baptism in the New Testament and Its Cultural Settings," *Worship and Culture in Dialog,* ed. S. Anita Stauffer (Geneva: The Lutheran World Federation, 1994), p. 17 n.2.

possibly be competent to make equally discerning judgment about every kind of music or art. Yet almost everyone is inclined to assume or act otherwise. That impulse is related to the sin of pride.

6. It is an act of Christian love to learn to appreciate or at least respect what others value in a particular style or work that they cherish in worship or in the rest of life. That is different, however, from personally liking every form of commendable art, which is impossible and unnecessary.

7. Disagreements over taste in religious music (or any other art) can be healthy and productive; but they touch on sensitive matters and often reflect or embody religious differences as well as aesthetic ones.

8. The reasons why an aesthetic work or style

is good or bad, weak or strong (and in what circumstances), can never be expressed fully in words; yet they can often be pointed out through comparative – and repeated – looking and listening.

9. Aesthetic judgments begin with, and owe special consideration to, the community or tradition to which a given style or work is indigenous or most familiar. But they seldom end there; and they cannot, if the style or work is to invite the attention of a wide range of people over a period of time.

10. The overall evaluation of any art used in worship needs to be a joint effort between clergy, congregation, and trained artists and musicians, taking into account not only the aesthetic qualities of the art itself but also the larger requirements and

continued . . .

Take, for example, the definition offered in 1973 by anthropologist Clifford Geertz. Says Geertz,

> the concept of culture I espouse . . . is essentially a semiotic one. Believing, with Max Weber, that man is an animal suspended in webs of significance he himself has spun, I take culture to be those webs, and the analysis of it to be therefore not an experimental science in search of law but an interpretive one in search of meaning.[9]

According to Geertz, what faces an anthropologist, or more specifically an ethnographer, when he engages a culture "is a multiplicity of complex conceptual structures, many of them superimposed upon or knotted into one another, which are at once strange, irregular, and inexplicit, and which he must contrive somehow first to grasp

9. Clifford Geertz, "Thick Description: Toward an Interpretive Theory of Culture," in *The Interpretation of Cultures: Selected Essays* (New York: Basic, 1973), p. 5.

contours of worship, which should at once respond to and orient the particular work of art or music.

11. While relative accessibility is imperative for most church art, the church also needs art — including "classic" art of various kinds — that continually challenges and solicits spiritual and theological growth in the aesthetic dimension. This is art that the Christian can grow into but seldom out of.

12. Almost every artistic style that has been enjoyed and valued by a particular group over a long period of time and for a wide range of purposes has religious potential. That is because life typically finds various and surprising ways of turning religious. As Augustine said, our hearts are restless until they rest in God.

Excerpt from *Good Taste, Bad Taste, and Christian Taste: Aesthetics in Religious Life* (New York: Oxford University Press, 2000), pp. 250-51.

---

and then to render."[10] To Geertz, culture is something of a text, and its analysis is a practice that is closer to the work of a literary critic than it is to that of cryptographer.[11] So "doing ethnography is like trying to read (in the sense of 'construct a reading of') a manuscript — foreign, faded, full of ellipses, incoherencies, suspicious emendations, and tendentious commentaries, . . . written . . . in transient examples of shaped behavior."[12] Culture is public, and public behavior must be attended to, says Geertz, because "it is through the flow of behavior — or more precisely, social action — that cultural forms find articulation."[13]

With that, Geertz commends his colleagues to do as he has done: to write about the entire scope of public behavior, about nationalism, violence, identity, human nature, legitimacy, revolution, ethnicity, urbanization, status, death, time, and especially about attempts among particular peoples to place such things in a meaningful frame.[14]

Concerning the scope of culture, H. Richard Niebuhr, a theologian, had come to a similar conclusion back in the 1950s. In his landmark lectures, *Christ and Culture*, Niebuhr defines culture broadly

10. Geertz, "Thick Description," p. 10.
11. Geertz, "Thick Description," p. 9.
12. Geertz, "Thick Description," p. 10.
13. Geertz, "Thick Description," p. 17.
14. Geertz, "Thick Description," p. 30.

as "the total process of human activity and the total result of such activity." He considers culture to be "the 'artificial, secondary environment'" that we humans superimpose, or overlay, upon the natural environment. As such, it includes every facet of our being and doing in the world: languages, habits, ideas, beliefs, customs, social organizations, values. Culture cannot be escaped. We are, in Niebuhr's estimation, "inevitably subject" to it.[15]

Finally, Clifford Orwin, a political theorist, bundles up all that can be said about culture into a single phrase. With reference to any people group, says Orwin, culture is "the totality of its social practices."[16] Such practices, of course, have to do with more than simple patterns of actions. They have to do with our every thought, word, and deed, their motivations and their manifestations.

Just from these definitions and descriptions we may infer a number of things about culture generally. For instance, we may infer that culture is an inevitable feature of human existence, and that it's pervasive, involving every aspect of our common life and extending well into every aspect of one's personal life.

Because culture is a social phenomenon, we speak of it with respect to "people groups." But people groups differ, just as individuals do, even within what one would call a single society. In their work in communication theory, Larry Samovar and Richard Porter explore these differences, suggesting that there are — within, say, North American society — a multiplicity of co-cultures, or "groups of people that exist within a society but outside the dominant culture."[17] Such groups — and there are many — include not only ethnic minorities and recent immigrants but also the deaf, the elderly, the homeless; even the incarcerated and gang members.[18] Accord-

---

15. H. Richard Niebuhr, *Christ and Culture* (New York: Harper and Row, 1951), p. 32.

16. Clifford Orwin, "All Quiet on the (Post) Western Front?" *The Public Interest* 123 (Spring 1996): 3-21.

17. Larry A. Samovar and Richard E. Porter, *Communication between Cultures* (Belmont, Calif.: Wadsworth, 1991), p. 158. This idea of co-cultures is valuable, even for those who do not follow Samovar and Porter's distinction between dominant and nondominant culture.

18. Samovar and Porter, *Communication between Cultures*, pp. 159ff.

ing to Samovar and Porter, groups like these often develop their own patterns of speech that simultaneously arise from and give rise to a unique cultural milieu.

Suppose we allow that as a society North America does comprise an array of people groups, or co-cultures. And suppose we assume that each group's values, rhetoric, and practices differ, sometimes subtly and sometimes significantly. It's fairly obvious that in North America, these co-cultures overlap and interact, such that on any given day any one of us may find ourselves having existed for a time in a culture other than the one that might be, so to speak, our *own* cultural identity. This might be so just because we regularly ride public transit from our south suburban home through the inner city to our downtown office. Or because a favorite lunch spot is that little storefront restaurant in the heart of Chinatown.

From the definitions above we may infer that human culture is not only multiple but also dynamic. Social practices are always evolving — out of all that they inherit from the past, with all that they absorb in the present, into something of what they will be in the future, whether that is in a year, a decade, or a century. This evolution occurs not just because time is passing, but because these co-cultures keep interacting. MTV culture, for example, is bred from "rock music, popular movies, and live and recorded television programming," innovatively combined with commercial advertising.[19] Back in the 1980s, when it first appeared, "MTV was not so much a new medium as a synthesis of styles and know-how from many media,"[20] which were and are themselves still evolving.

So culture is, in some sense, the dynamic totality of our habitual, or nearly habitual, ways of being and doing in the world. Such an understanding of culture lands us very near Orwin's: culture has to do with our daily practices, our considered and unconsidered routines. It has to do with the way we measure time, prepare food, and

19. Quentin J. Schultze et al., *Dancing in the Dark: Youth, Popular Culture, and the Electronic Media* (Grand Rapids: Eerdmans, 1991), p. 180.
20. Schultze et al., *Dancing in the Dark*, p. 180.

discipline children. It has to do with the way we receive information, guests, and gifts; the way we express opinions, emotions, and thoughts; the way we rest, rise, and recreate. It also has to do with the way we worship — what, when, and where.

This is why in planning and leading worship, church leaders are constantly answering questions (even if they aren't consciously *asking* questions) about culture when they adopt a certain leadership style, or when they choose what to wear on Sunday morning and whether to change clothes between the "traditional" and "contemporary" services.

Cultural Adaptation of Worship Is Inevitable

If Niebuhr is right in saying that we are "inevitably subject" to culture, then it stands to reason that our social habits and practices will naturally be subject to adaptation as they are expressed by one people group as opposed to another. And so it has been with worship, and not just worship, but also the very gospel that inspires it.

Cultural adaptation has been a feature of the gospel ever since it was received in the first century A.D. Consider the fact that we have not one, but four accounts of Christ's ministry, death, and resurrection — four accounts, each of which is itself a cultural adaptation. For instance, Matthew addressed his Gospel to kindred Palestinian Jews. Since Aramaic would be familiar to his primary readers, he doesn't translate every Aramaic quotation into Greek, as Mark does in his book. Matthew also emphasizes Jesus' lineage and the fulfillment of Old Testament prophecy in him. Luke, however, wrote his Gospel primarily for fellow Greek-speaking Gentiles, as is evidenced by his address to Theophilus. The introduction of Luke's Gospel is stylistically Greco-Roman, and throughout his narrative, Luke persists in demonstrating the relevance of Christ for the salvation even of those outside Israel.[21]

---

21. See D. A. Carson et al., *An Introduction to the New Testament* (Grand Rapids: Zondervan, 1992).

Church and Mission "According to the Whole"

Justo L. González

[In *Translating the Message: The Missionary Impact on Culture* (Maryknoll, N.Y.: Orbis, 1989), Lamin Sanneh writes:]

There are two basic ways to proceed. One is to make the missionary culture the inseparable carrier of the message. This we might call mission by *diffusion*. By it religion expands from its original cultural base and is implanted in other societies primarily as a matter of cultural identity. Islam, with which Christianity shares a strong missionary tradition, exemplifies this mode of mission. It carries with it certain inalienable cultural assumptions, such as the indispensability of its Arabic heritage in Scripture, law and religion.

The other way is to make the recipient culture the true and final locus of the proclamation, so that the religion arrives without the presumption of cultural rejection. This we might call mission by *translation*. It carries with it a deep theological vocation, which arises as an inevitable stage in the process of reception and adaptation. [p. 27]

These contrasting approaches to mission stem from different views on the nature of sacred Scripture: the Koran is a single book; the Bible is a series of books and includes a variety of perspectives and interpretations of the events with which it deals.

Christianity is based on the fourfold witness to the gospel, and on a Bible that includes a similar

---

But what about these smatterings of Aramaic in the Gospels? It seems Jesus often preached in Aramaic, talked with his disciples in Aramaic, and charged the dead to rise and evil spirits to come out — in Aramaic. Yet these events were recorded in Greek, not, apparently, because Greek was an inherently superior language, but because it was the broadband signal of the Greco-Roman world, the language of commerce, politics, and education, and so of Christianity.[22] (This meant that, already in the first century, many believers engaged in a cross-cultural experience whenever they heard the gospel read: Either they were Greek hearing a Greek record of Semitic experience, or they were Semitic hearing of Semitic experience in a Greek record, or they were neither Greek nor Semitic and thus

22. Gerard Mussies, "Greek As the Vehicle for Early Christianity," *New Testament Studies* 29, no. 3 (July 1983): 356-69.

diversity of perspectives. For such a religion, "catholicity" is crucial, and this catholicity means, not only being present throughout the world, but also being a faith "according to the whole" – meaning, in the New Testament, according to the whole witness of all four evangelists, and, in the best times of its history, according to the perspective, experience, and witness of all the *oikoumene.*

In brief, the Christian missionary enterprise is based on two poles, both equally important, but one often forgotten. On the one hand – and this has been emphasized most often – the Christian missionary enterprise is based on the need of "the nations." As Christians, we are convinced that the gospel is indeed Good News that all should hear, and which we must proclaim to all. On the other hand, the Christian missionary enterprise is also based on the catholic vocation of the gospel. To

paraphrase Irenaeus, just as there are four gospels which in their multiplicity witness to the one gospel, it is necessary that believers from all the four corners of the earth bring the richness of their experience and perception of the gospel, so that we may all come to a fuller, more "catholic" – "according to the whole" – understanding of the gospel. The church calls all the "nations" to the gospel, not only because the "nations" need the gospel, but also because the church needs the "nations" in order to be fully "catholic." If "catholic" means "according to the whole," as long as a part of the whole remains outside, or is brought in without being allowed to speak from its own perspective, catholicity itself is truncated.

Excerpt from *Out of Every Tribe and Nation* (Nashville: Abingdon, 1992), pp. 28-29.

---

underwent a cross-cultural experience both ways. We undergo the same cross-cultural experience, except that we are distanced not only by ethnic background but also by time.) Then down through the ages and across the continents the church itself has translated the gospel into hundreds of languages, following the precedent of Pentecost in order to fulfill the great commission (Acts 2:5-6; Matt. 28:19; Luke 24:47; Acts 1:8).

Like the gospel (and the Gospels), worship, too, has been "translated" down through the ages and across the continents. It, too, has been culturally adapted. If you think about it, every form of worship in the world today is a "translation" of what has come before, whether it's so-called "traditional" or "contemporary." This has been so throughout history.

Already in the first century, worship was practiced in several languages: Coptic, Syriac, Aramaic, and Greek, just to name a few. Eventually communities of believers wrote down their prayers and their formulas for baptism and Eucharist, sharing them from church to church and reciting them from year to year. By the third century, churches to the west, especially in North Africa, began using Latin in worship, first for Scripture readings, then for prayers, then for baptism and Eucharist. In time, these churches developed their own prayers and expressions for worship, reflecting a distinctly Roman literary style, rich with rhetorical novelty.[23] Rhythm and end rhyme conveyed as much praise or lament as the very words themselves.

Or consider the Lord's Supper. Scripture's cue seems simple: churches should serve unleavened bread and wine. But even food is culturally conditioned. Different foods mean different things in different cultures, and so with regard to the bread and wine, fitting substitutions have been introduced. In some Asian countries, rice cakes and tea are served for the holy supper.[24] In North America, back in the mid 1800s, hundreds of folk, including many Christians, rallied under the banner of temperance. In order that churches might also comply, Dr. Thomas Bramwell Welch, a dentist by profession and the steward of Communion in a Methodist church, pasteurized Concord grape juice to produce "an unfermented sacramental wine."[25]

> "Preaching is finally more than art or science. It is alchemy, in which tin becomes gold and yard rocks become diamonds under the influence of the Holy Spirit. It is a process of transformation for both preacher and congregation alike, as the ordinary details of their everyday lives are translated into extraordinary elements of God's ongoing creation."
>
> Barbara Brown Taylor, *The Preaching Life* (Cambridge, Mass.: Cowley, 1993), pp. 85-86

---

23. Anscar Chupungco, "Eucharist in the Early Church and Its Cultural Settings," *Worship and Culture in Dialog*, ed. S. Anita Stauffer (Geneva: The Lutheran World Federation, 1994), pp. 87ff.

24. Robert E. Webber, ed., *The Ministries of Christian Worship*, vol. 7 of The Complete Library of Christian Worship (Nashville: Star Song, 1994), p. 220.

25. Betty O. O'Brien, "The Lord's Supper: Fruit of the Vine or Cup of Devils?" *Methodist History* 31, no. 4 (July 1993): 203-33.

Of course, music has been "translated" down through the centuries, too. The church of the first seven centuries was a singing church, though we don't really know what their psalms, hymns, and antiphons sounded like. More familiar to the church is the music that has come along since: Gregorian, Byzantine, and Russian chant; eight-part motets; organ chorale preludes; Genevan psalm tunes; English anthems; Wesley-brother hymns; ring shouts; camp meeting spirituals; shape-note folk tunes; Southern gospel songs. Even jazz riffs, mariachi trumpets, Irish mandolins, and Balinese gamelans.

So, as with culture itself, the cultural adaptation of worship appears to be inevitable. Why? For one thing, Scripture gives little guidance as to how worship ought to take place and how it ought to progress. While the Old Testament is replete with ritual detail, Christ himself told us that he, through his death and resurrection, is the fulfillment of these laws. So the ceremonies they govern are no longer binding, no longer appropriate, except as redefined through Christ. And Christ did redefine two rituals, namely, baptism and the Lord's Supper, as the successors of circumcision and the Passover. Still, unlike the Old Testament, the New Testament doesn't provide detailed instruction for the sacraments (How much water? What kind of bread?), and doesn't tell us much with respect to worship either.

In Luke's account of Pentecost and in Paul's letter to the Corinthians we get glimpses, at most. There we find that believers gathered for the preaching of the word, the breaking of bread, praying, singing, and the sharing of all things in common (Acts 2; 1 Cor. 14:26). But exactly how did these first-century Christians do these things? And supposing we knew how they did them, what would that mean for how twenty-first-century Christians should do them? As just noted, the New Testament hardly provides a prescription for what *must* take place in worship, in what order, or in what manner. The author of Hebrews encourages believers "not to give up meeting together," and Paul urges them to do that which is "fitting and orderly" when they do meet together. Here, Paul's words fall upon our ears

**Excerpts from the Nairobi Statement
on Worship and Culture**
Lutheran World Federation

2. Worship as Transcultural

2.1. The resurrected Christ whom we worship, and through whom by the power of the Holy Spirit we know the grace of the Triune God, transcends and indeed is beyond all cultures. In the mystery of his resurrection is the source of the transcultural nature of Christian worship. Baptism and Eucharist, the sacraments of Christ's death and resurrection, were given by God for all the world. There is one Bible, translated into many tongues, and biblical preaching of Christ's death and resurrection has been sent into all the world. The fundamental shape of the principal Sunday act of Christian worship, the Eucharist or Holy Communion, is shared across cultures: the people

gather, the Word of God is proclaimed, the people intercede for the needs of the Church and the world, the eucharistic meal is shared, and the people are sent out into the world for mission. The great narratives of Christ's birth, death, resurrection, and sending of the Spirit, and our Baptism into him, provide the central meanings of the transcultural times of the church's year: especially Lent/Easter/Pentecost, and, to a lesser extent, Advent/Christmas/Epiphany. The ways in which the shapes of the Sunday Eucharist and the church year are expressed vary by culture, but their meanings and fundamental structure are shared around the globe. There is one Lord, one faith, one Baptism, one Eucharist.

2.2. Several specific elements of Christian liturgy are also transcultural, e.g., readings from the Bible . . . , the ecumenical creeds and the Our Father, and Baptism in water in the Triune Name.

---

as a license, but one that assumes responsibility. That is to say, Paul licenses not just *anything* for worship, but what is *fitting* for worship.

What does that mean? Today we find ourselves preaching the gospel and worshiping God in contemporary North American culture. As we saw earlier, North American culture comprises many cultures, though as a whole it's variously purported to be postmodern, post-literate, pre-Christian, post-Christian, relativistic, subjectivistic, materialistic, experiential, sensorial, and the list goes on. What does it mean to proclaim the gospel in *this* culture? What does it mean to "sing the Lord's song" in *this* foreign land?

It's clear, for example, that we can't do as Jesus did by preaching in Aramaic. That language has been dead for at least six centuries. During the Second Vatican Council, prelates acknowledged that

2.3. The use of this shared core liturgical structure and these shared liturgical elements in local congregational worship . . . are expressions of Christian unity across time, space, culture, and confession. The recovery in each congregation of the clear centrality of these transcultural and ecumenical elements renews the sense of this Christian unity and gives all churches a solid basis for authentic contextualization.

3. Worship as Contextual

3.1. Jesus whom we worship was born into a specific culture of the world. In the mystery of his incarnation are the model and the mandate for the contextualization of Christian worship. God can be and is encountered in the local cultures of our world. A given culture's values and patterns, insofar as they are consonant with the values of the Gospel, can be used to express the meaning and purpose of Christian worship. Contextualization is a necessary task for the Church's mission in the world, so that the Gospel can be ever more deeply rooted in diverse local cultures.

3.2. Among the various methods of contextualization, that of dynamic equivalence is particularly useful. It involves re-expressing components of Christian worship with something from a local culture that has an equal meaning, value, and function. Dynamic equivalence goes far beyond mere translation; it involves understanding the fundamental meanings both of elements of worship and of the local culture, and enabling the meanings and actions of worship to be "encoded" and re-expressed in the language of local culture. . . .

continued . . .

---

conducting the Mass in Latin wasn't particularly communicative throughout the world either, so they allowed a more extended use of native languages in local parishes.

Like the language in which we hear the gospel proclaimed, the tonality and rhythmic inflection of the "psalms, hymns, and spiritual songs" with which we respond will also depend upon our cultural particularity. Our ethnic background and regional locale and socioeconomic niche — these things, among others, influence how we worship, and where, and when, because they've influenced who we are.

Cultural adaptation of worship is inevitable, even as we are "inevitably subject" to culture. So if worship isn't adapted to *this* culture — including, to some measure, contemporary popular culture — it's not that it is being adapted to *no* culture, but to some other one.

3.4. Local churches might also consider the method of creative assimilation. . . . Unlike dynamic equivalence, creative assimilation enriches the liturgical ordo — not by culturally re-expressing its elements, but by adding to it new elements from local culture.

3.5. In contextualization the fundamental values and meanings both of Christianity and of local cultures must be respected.

3.6. An important criterion for dynamic equivalence and creative assimilation is that sound or accepted liturgical traditions are preserved in order to keep unity with the universal Church's tradition of worship, while progress inspired by pastoral needs is encouraged. On the side of culture, it is understood that not everything can be integrated with Christian worship, but only those elements that are connatural to (that is, of the same nature as) the liturgical

ordo. Elements borrowed from local culture should always undergo critique and purification, which can be achieved through the use of biblical typology.

4. Worship as Counter-Cultural

4.1. Jesus Christ came to transform all people and all cultures, and calls us not to conform to the world, but to be transformed with it (Rom. 12:2). In the mystery of his passage from death to eternal life is the model for transformation, and thus for the counter-cultural nature of Christian worship. Some components of every culture in the world are sinful, dehumanizing, and contradictory to the values of the Gospel. From the perspective of the Gospel, they need critique and transformation. Contextualization of Christian faith and worship necessarily involves challenging of all types of

---

Worship doesn't take shape in a cultural vacuum, for culture is the gospel's atmosphere, worship's habitat.[26]

CULTURAL ADAPTATION OF WORSHIP IS DESIRABLE

Given these facts, it turns out that the cultural adaptation of worship is not only inevitable but also desirable. For one thing, translation and adaptation are useful for evangelism. Reflect again on Pentecost and the centuries-long practice of translating the gospel that it began. Just as people ought to hear the gospel in a culturally perceptible

26. John D. Witvliet, "Theological and Conceptual Models for Liturgy and Culture," *Liturgy Digest* 3, no. 2 (1996): 35-36.

oppression and social injustice wherever they exist in earthly cultures.

4.2. It also involves the transformation of cultural patterns which idolize the self or the local group at the expense of a wider humanity, or which give central place to the acquisition of wealth at the expense of the care of the earth and its poor. The tools of the counter-cultural in Christian worship may also include the deliberate maintenance or recovery of patterns of action which differ intentionally from prevailing cultural models. These patterns may arise from a recovered sense of Christian history, or from the wisdom of other cultures.

5. Worship as Cross-Cultural

5.1. Jesus came to be the Savior of all people. He welcomes the treasures of earthly cultures into the city of God. By virtue of Baptism, there is one Church; and one means of living in faithful response to Baptism is to manifest ever more deeply the unity of the Church. The sharing of hymns and art and other elements of worship across cultural barriers helps enrich the whole Church and strengthen the sense of the communio of the Church. This sharing can be ecumenical as well as cross-cultural, as a witness to the unity of the Church and the oneness of Baptism. Cross-cultural sharing is possible for every church, but is especially needed in multicultural congregations and member churches.

5.2. Care should be taken that the music, art, architecture, gestures and postures, and other elements of different cultures are understood and respected when they are used by churches elsewhere in the

continued . . .

---

form, that is, in their native language, so also they ought to worship in one. This "ought" is only natural. It's only natural for the church to be culturally astute and then to practice its worship accordingly. Simply put, this keeps worshipers from stumbling over unnecessary obstacles, and helps them engage God more directly. (The question remains for later discussion whether there are any "necessary obstacles" that should be retained in Christian worship.)

For instance, what if the gospel reaches an indigenous people for whom immersing, dousing, or even sprinkling another's head is taboo? What if such an action signifies a curse?[27] In such cultures

27. Such is the case with the Masai people of Africa. Pouring water over a woman's head is a ritual cursing her to barrenness. R. Schreiter, *Constructing Local Theology* (Maryknoll, N.Y.: Orbis, 1985), p. 2, cited in Stephen B. Bevans, *Models of Contextual Theology* (Maryknoll, N.Y.: Orbis, 1992), p. 6.

world. The criteria for contextualization (above, sections 3.5 and 3.6) should be observed.

6. Challenge to the Churches

6.1. We call on all member churches of the Lutheran World Federation to undertake more efforts related to the transcultural, contextual, counter-cultural, and cross-cultural nature of Christian worship. We call on all member churches to recover the centrality of Baptism, Scripture with preaching, and the every-Sunday celebration of the Lord's Supper — the principal transcultural elements of Christian worship and the signs of Christian unity — as the strong center of all congregational life and mission, and as the authentic basis for contextualization. We call on all churches to give serious attention to exploring the local or contextual elements of liturgy, language, posture and gesture, hymnody and other music and musical instruments, and art and architecture for Christian worship — so that their worship may be more truly rooted in the local culture. We call those churches now carrying out missionary efforts to encourage such contextual awareness among themselves and also among the partners and recipients of their ministries. [And] we call on all member churches to give serious attention to the transcultural nature of worship and the possibilities for cross-cultural sharing. . . .

Reprinted by permission of the Department for Theology and Studies of the Lutheran World Federation (LWF).

---

adaptation of Christian baptism is warranted. Perhaps water will be poured over the believer's shoulders, and the sign of the cross will be marked on her forehead with a dry hand.

In a remote village in the Southern Highlands of Papua New Guinea, the Obene people have built an elaborate bamboo pipeline to supply their baptismal water. Resting on stilts, the pipeline extends from the top of a hill, presumably from a freshwater stream, to the village below. Its end is near their church's altar, and from it flows a small waterfall. During baptism, new believers, young and old alike, stand beneath the falling water while a minister announces their baptism in the name of the Father, the Son, and the Holy Spirit. It's fitting to be baptized in this "living water," say the Obene people, and not the "plastic water" that they carry in a jug.[28]

In his book *Beyond the Worship Wars: Building Vital and Faithful Wor-*

28. Thomas Kane, *The Dancing Church of the South Pacific* (Mahwah, N.J.: Paulist, 1998), videorecording.

ship, Thomas G. Long tells of an African-American church in Chicago that involves whole families, including the family of God, in their services of "baby dedication." At the appointed time in worship, the minister invites the families of the children to come forward. The minister blesses each child, turning first to the mother, who recites the child's first name, then to the father, who recites the child's middle name, then to the child's whole family — siblings, grandparents, aunts, uncles, and cousins, gathered in the front of the church — who shout the last name.

After the pastor blesses the last child, African drums are sounded. The parents with their babies march to the polyrhythmic beat across the front of the sanctuary and up the steps onto the chancel platform. Shouting with praise and thanksgiving, the congregation adds their voice to the persistent rhythms. Recalls Long:

> When the parents and their children were arrayed across the chancel and as the drums continued to strike the rhythm, a team of women, lay worship leaders, began to move from child to child, each woman carrying something to place in the mouths of the babies. The first woman placed a bit of pepper in each baby's mouth, and as she did a woman at the lectern said, "This pepper is a sign of the power of the cross." The next woman put a drop of water in each mouth. "This water is a sign of the purity of Christ, to whom this child belongs." The next woman placed a pinch of salt on the tongues of the children. "This salt is a sign that these children are called to be wise and faithful, the salt of the earth." The next woman carried drops of vinegar, and the babies winced. "This vinegar is a sign that the Christian life will not always be easy and that these children must be prepared to face difficulties and suffering." The next a bit of honey. "A sign of the sweetness of the Gospel." The last woman carried oil. "A sign of joy."
>
> When the women had finished, the drums grew very loud, the congregation rose with acclamations to its feet, and the parents lifted up each child as high as they could over their heads as the

woman at the lectern announced with joyful triumph, "These children were not born into slavery. They are the free children of the heavenly King, those loved and chosen by God most High!"[29]

For worship to take shape in so many culturally enriched forms is for worship to reflect the glory of God, to display the very complexion of God's creation. Instead of just one species of fish, God caused more than 220 species to flourish in the mangrove swamps of southern Florida alone. Throughout the world, there are better than 700,000 species of insects and 250,000 varieties of plants. Indeed, says Calvin, "wherever you cast your eyes, there is no spot in the universe wherein you cannot discern at least some sparks of [God's] glory."[30] And so it is with culture. The very variety that characterizes the natural world also characterizes the peoples given a home in it.

There are many cultures, but there is one Spirit, who hovers over the face of the earth. Over regions the gospel has not yet reached, the Spirit still broods, bestowing God's grace in various forms. Though not salvific, such grace is common to Jew and Greek, male and female, barbarian, Scythian, slave, and free. God's grace "makes his sun rise on the evil and on the good, and sends rain on the righteous and on the unrighteous" (Matt. 5:45). God's grace sustains, even within those who seem "least to differ from brutes" (as Calvin describes them), a *sensus divinitatis,* a sense of the divine, which itself preserves something of a religious worldview and godly conscience.[31] Common grace may have the effect of a primer, preparing a people for the gift of the gospel. It may yield cultural events, practices, ideas — or an "unknown god" like the one Paul discovered at the Areopagus — to which the gospel might attach. These things are of God, though they might not first appear so.

29. Thomas G. Long, *Beyond the Worship Wars: Building Vital and Faithful Worship* (Bethesda, Md.: Alban Institute, 2001), pp. 50-51.

30. John Calvin, *Institutes of the Christian Religion,* 2 vols., ed. John T. McNeill, trans. Ford Lewis Battles (Philadelphia: Westminster, 1960), 1:52 (1.5.1).

31. Calvin, *Institutes* 1:43-44 (1.3.1).

So no culture is devoid of God's grace. But then no culture, or even cultural practice, is devoid of sin either. The former allows for the cultural adaptation of worship, while the latter makes it risky.

Cultural Adaptation of Worship Is Risky

We've already identified the major risk: translation, or adaptation, can by itself mislead us. New words may subvert the intent of original ones. That is, whether we're dealing with Scripture or worship, we might distort or even lose the gospel in translation by adding a foreign ingredient or subtracting an essential one.

For example, some Contemporary Worship leaders "host" their worship in the style of late-night TV talk show comedians. Either naturally or intentionally they are picking up the tenor of a prominent segment of popular culture marked by a tone of detached irony. Accordingly, the reading of Scripture may be interjected with editorial comment: "if you will not listen to me . . . then I will do this to you [Listen up, y'all]: I will bring upon you sudden terror, wasting diseases and fever [Sounds like *fun*, doesn't it?]. . . ."

A question arises: Does such rhetoric subvert the seriousness of Scripture and the reverence believers owe it?

A second question: What about the music to which we sing the Lord's song?

Throughout the history of the world, philosophers, revolutionaries, and theologians alike have reflected on music's power to *move* us. Somehow it reaches our inner being. And so Plato notes that harmony used well can settle one's soul,[32] but used wrongly can unsettle a whole society.[33] Aristotle also notes an affinity between

---

32. Plato, *Timaeus* 47e, in *The Collected Dialogues of Plato Including the Letters*, ed. Edith Hamilton and Huntington Cairns, trans. Lane Cooper et al. (New York: Pantheon, 1961), p. 1175.

33. Plato, *Republic* 424b-c, in *Collected Dialogues of Plato*, pp. 665-66.

Preaching in an Anti-Authority Age

Duane K. Kelderman

How does the Christian preacher proclaim God's Word with authority in a culture that doesn't much believe in authority? In our postmodern society, no one seems to be sure of anything, and making an authoritative claim to the truth seems almost quaint. The prevailing ethos of our culture suggests that "truth" in life is your truth and my truth and their truth, but no overarching, transcendent truth. In this environment, any religion that declares its truth in a way that judges another religion to be in error is somewhere between arrogant and oppressive.

So how does the Christian preacher proclaim God's Word in this sort of world? I would suggest that the Christian message has more possibilities in this anti-authority culture than one might think.

For starters, *the challenge posed by our culture is really nothing new.* Authority has never had an easy time. Here we might clarify what we mean by authority. Authority is a combination of *power* and *legitimacy.* It is not merely power. Authority also entails a legitimacy established by

character and competence. Jesus taught as one having authority, but he was not *authoritarian.* He did not rule by coercion (power). No, he was a person of authority, whom people respected and followed because of the depth of his wisdom and the strength of his character (legitimacy).

Innovative church leaders today often pit authority against authenticity. They argue that people today do not listen to pastors merely because they are authority figures but because they authentically embody the message (if in fact the ministers do). On one level, the observation of these church leaders has always been true. The burden that those in authority have for establishing their authority has always been a heavy one. True, our culture makes it tougher for those in authority to gain a hearing. But this is not a new problem. It's only a variation on a theme.

Second, Christian preachers should be encouraged by the fact that *while people in our culture dismiss authority, they still long for some authoritative center in their lives.* While the spirit of the age may be anti-authority, people today are searching for meaning and wholeness in their lives. One need merely

---

the soul and harmony, but unlike Plato, more fully appreciates its entertainments. Still, says Aristotle, there's a right time and a right place for the right harmony.[34]

These themes are sounded in the early church, too, by Basil,

34. Aristotle, *The Politics,* trans. T. S. Sinclair, revised and re-presented by Trevor J. Saunders (Harmondsworth: Penguin Classics, revised ed. 1981), p. 316, in *Music in the Western World: A History in Documents,* selected and annotated by Piero Weiss and Richard Taruskin (New York: Schirmer, 1984), p. 12.

scan the self-help titles in a bookstore to see that this is so. The fact that young people in our culture tend to distrust traditional centers of authority, and even deny the possibility of knowing or asserting anything with certainty, is very different from saying they do not seek some authoritative center to their lives. We still long for meaning that comes from beyond us.

Third, *Christian preachers can be encouraged because they represent a faith that is not an authoritarian one.* The Christian religion is not a coercive religion, demanding blind conformity from its adherents. The Good News is freely offered; people freely choose to accept or reject it. The best of Christian preaching does not manipulate its listeners, forcing them where they would not otherwise go. It persuades its listeners to come to the foot of the cross, to Christ.

Much of our cultural resistance to authority is not really a resistance to fitting authority but a resistance to abuses of authority. Unfortunately, Christianity is often characterized as being *inherently* abusive, manipulative, and authoritarian — a squelcher of personal freedom. This simply is not true, and Christians must press for a fairer hearing from those who identify Christianity with authoritarian excess.

Fourth, *the Christian religion is well-suited for our culture's cry for authenticity, not authority.* Study after study asserts that Gen-Xers are unimpressed with authority figures but demand authenticity: "Show me you are for real." Compared to anything else our world has to offer, Christianity, whose centerpiece is the incarnation of God in Christ, puts on a radical "show." The entire biblical drama is the story of an all-powerful God who does not rule by fiat from a distance, but who comes near in servant love, and by his incarnate presence enables us to see God (John 1:18). Christians need not resist the "show me" demands of a generation skeptical of authority.

Christian preaching is first of all a witness, a testimony to what God has done and is doing in history, of what God's children have seen and heard. Some innovative church leaders argue that propositions and dogma are out today, and that narrative and testimony are in. This suits the Christian tradition just fine. The authority of Christian preaching derives from God and what God has

continued . . .

Chrysostom, Origen, and Augustine. Augustine delights to hear singing in worship, in part because it is so moving. Yet he worries that the singing is sometimes more moving than the truth it's meant to convey. At those times, says Augustine, "I would prefer not to have heard the singer."[35]

The Reformers also recognized the power of music to move us.

35. Augustine, *Confessions,* trans. and with an intro. by Henry Chadwick (New York: Oxford, 1992), p. 208 (10.33.50).

done in history. The content of Christian faith is narrative at its core. Christian preachers simply tell the story of what they have seen and heard (and doctrine is helpful when it explains the meaning of these historical actions). Paul's and Peter's preaching in Acts was not argumentative as much as it was personal testimony.

A related feature of Christian preaching that fits well in our "show me," anti-authority culture is its willingness to be tested and approved in the lives of its listeners. Christians do not fear the reality test. A helpful way to focus this approach in preaching is to ask: Is something true because it's in the Bible, or is something in the Bible because it's true? Adultery isn't wrong *first of all* because it says so in the Bible; it's wrong because it doesn't work, it doesn't fit with how God created human beings to function. The Bible simply names what is already so. Christians believe that the Christian faith is the most complete and best explanation of reality, and that resonates with those who expect the validation of truth in experience.

Finally, *Christian preaching is well-suited to our anti-authority culture because of its ability to relate to a suffering world.* For all of its prosperity, North America is a society of sufferers. A prosperous society creates its own kind of anxiety — of getting, keeping, and spending. The breakdown of marriage and family has resulted in an increased number of people, especially younger people, experiencing traumatic pain and brokenness. Substance abuse, eating disorders, gambling addiction, compulsive behaviors (like workaholism) — all are evidence of an addictive quality in North American life, and all are related to pain. North Americans are overly busy, stressed, tired — never "unhooked" in an instant society with its cell phones, pagers, e-mail, and voicemail. According to most surveys, Americans are not happy or fulfilled.

In this context, Christian preachers "know what time it is." They know that we have not entered the Promised Land yet, and that we ought not claim too much for this world. Our eschatological situation calls for preaching that not only declares what God in Christ has already now done and echoes the promises of what he has not yet done, but also gives voice to human suffering and the ongoing brokenness of life.

So along with their gladness for music's power to penetrate our hearts and to lift them up in more fervent praise to God, they also expressed caution. In one breath Luther extols music's virtue, in that it may incline us to goodness by the prodding of the Spirit, and in the next breath warns of its vice, in that it may incline us to evil by the goading of the devil. So "take special care," wrote Luther, "to shun perverted minds who prostitute this lovely gift of nature and art with their erotic rantings," for such folk "defy

Preaching that is sensitive to suffering fits in a culture where listeners resist superficial, easy answers to life's problems. People long for a framework within which they can at least name their pain and suffering. The Christian message has a place for suffering. It is a gospel of the cross, not just the empty tomb. It has a place for searching, for lamenting, for grieving. The Christian religion is not only an "already now" religion; it's also a "not yet" religion.

At a time when many Christians fear that our anti-authority culture simply takes away the possibility of the Christian religion receiving a meaningful hearing, we must realize the many ways that this simply is not so. This note of confidence should not, however, be construed as an invitation to careless communication to our culture. Christian preachers must work hard to avoid being misunderstood by those who suspect or reject the authoritative claims of Christianity. The church must design its ministry in such a way that the skeptic can experience Christ in Christian community even as she hears the Word she finds so difficult to accept. In this regard, many innovative church leaders have served the church well, pointing out the way more traditional churches may be maintaining unnecessary barriers to communication.

At the same time, Christians must confidently proclaim that Jesus Christ is Lord, fully realizing that this declaration assaults, head on, contrary beliefs about authority in our culture. The Christian preacher cannot ultimately avoid the offense of declaring that the Christian message is true, and true in such a way that it judges many other messages, even religious ones. In a culture where truth is relative, Christian preachers must have basic confidence in the message they preach.

The best Christian preaching is both careful and confident: careful to use language that is sensitive to cultural barriers to the gospel, and confident that the Holy Spirit may break through these barriers to create living faith. The challenge for the church in North America is to be concerned with contextualizing the gospel, but not so over-concerned that it loses confidence in the gospel.

---

their very nature which would and should praise God its Maker with this gift."[36] Calvin assumed a similar position. "In truth," says Calvin, "we know from experience that song has a great power and strength to move and inflame the hearts of men to invoke and

36. Martin Luther, in a preface written for the publication of a collection of Latin motets. Martin Luther, Preface to the *Synphoniae jucudae* (1538), trans. Ulrich S. Leupold, in *Luther's Works*, vol. 53 (Philadelphia: Fortress, 1964), as found in *Music in the Western World*, pp. 101-3.

praise God with a heart more vehement and ardent." But if that's so, then so is this: "just as wine is funneled into a barrel, so are venom and corruption distilled to the very depths of the heart by melody."[37]

Music moves us, or at least it has a powerful potential to do so. And so does God, who sometimes uses music as his instrument. But, as Hendrikus Berkhof's work suggests, God does not always move us, not even in worship; and not all that moves us is of God.[38] In a world where the prince of darkness masquerades as an angel of light, we do well to be discerning: are we really singing the Lord's song, or just another rendition of the Babylonian national anthem? What is moving us, and to where?

We need not stop with these examples. We could speak of architecture, lights, dance, inclusive language, and the visual arts. With each example, there are hard questions to be raised, but they all distill to this one: are we being faithful to the gospel, or are we betraying it by adding something to or subtracting something from its good news, even if inadvertently?

CULTURAL ADAPTATION: SEEKING THE WISDOM OF THE WORD

If cultural adaptation is so risky and the gift of discernment so necessary, where can we turn for guidance? What source may we plumb for wisdom? Scripture, of course. But what do Scripture's unfolding

---

37. John Calvin in his preface to the 1543 Genevan Psalter. Jean Calvin, *Oeuvres choisies* (Geneva: Chouet & Cie., 1909), pp. 173-76, as found in *Music in the Western World*, pp. 107-8. The fact that Luther wrote his comments in the preface to a collection of motets and that Calvin wrote his in the preface to the Genevan Psalter is telling. Luther and Calvin certainly held different views about music in worship, but similar views about its effects.

38. This point is Thomas G. Long's, derived from his reading of Hendrikus Berkhof, *Christian Faith: An Introduction to the Study of the Faith* (Grand Rapids: Eerdmans, 1979), p. 17. See Thomas G. Long, *Beyond the Worship Wars*, p. 32.

The Commercial Connection

Robb Redman

"The business of America," said President Calvin Coolidge, "is business."

Since the 1980s, the business of many Christians has been the production of Christian worship music. It is difficult to understand the current worship awakening without taking into account the role of the contemporary Christian music industry.

This industry has developed two distinct though related kinds of Christian music. The first is Contemporary Christian Music (CCM), whose industry is based primarily in Nashville. Among the best-known CCM artists today are Amy Grant, Michael W. Smith, DC Talk, Jars of Clay, and Steven Curtis Chapman, all of whom have had success on the "secular" pop charts. Their songs are primarily aimed at the listener, and they usually include either personal testimony or reflection on social or cultural themes. The other kind of Christian music is Contemporary Worship Music (CWM). This kind of music is directed primarily to God. Lyrics may be composed for congregational use or to express the devotion of the artist. In worship, this latter style leads the hearer in worship as choral anthems might in a more traditional setting. Maranatha! Music, Integrity Music, and Vineyard Music Group (known as The Big Three) are among the best-known producers of CWM, accounting for more than 80 percent of the CCLI (Christian Copyright Licensing Incorporated) Top 100 Praise and Worship songs.

In the early years of contemporary Christian music, artists and producers did not distinguish between message music and worship music. Concerts and recordings by groups of the 1970s —

continued . . .

events and recurring themes teach us about the cultural adaptation of the gospel and of worship?

We've already noted one relevant biblical event — Pentecost. On that great day, the Holy Spirit came in power and lit tongues of fire to inspire the tongues of apostles. The gospel that Jesus had proclaimed in Aramaic was now proclaimed by his followers at Pentecost, not in their own tongue, and not in an esoteric language of heaven, but in the indigenous languages of the earth — the *whole* earth, as far as the apostles were concerned. The miracle of Pentecost was meant not so much to dazzle the faithful as to signal the church's mission to "all who are far away, everyone whom the Lord our God calls to him" (Acts 2:39). Luke's use of the Greek word *makron* ("far away") tells us of people who particularly need the

Love Song, Second Chapter of Acts, John Fischer, and Phil Keaggy among others — freely mixed the two genres. The post–Love Song careers of Chuck Girard and Tommy Coomes illustrate the emerging distinction between the two: Girard continued to compose and perform message music; Coomes concentrated on worship music at his Calvary Chapel congregation in Costa Mesa. He recorded worship music albums for Maranatha! Music, eventually creating the Maranatha! Praise Band.

Since 1980, CWM has led to the formation of a significant production industry. The Big Three, other minor labels, CCM artists, independent producers, and even denominations are involved. While a number of CWM songs have entered the church through other means, most reach churches through commercial channels: CDs and sheet music, concerts and workshops.

Many critics of CWM argue that such music — having been marred by the secularism, consumerism, and materialism of the marketplace — is inappropriate for worship. The tension has been heightened in recent years as secular recording giants, such as EMI and BMG, have bought up CCM companies. To many, pitching worship songs as commodities demeans the music and the church. It treats believers as mere consumers. According to CWM's critics, believers should not entrust the production of worship music to companies whose bottom line is profit rather than the needs of congregations. This, they say, secularizes and corrupts CWM, which is therefore bound to be shallow, theologically weak, more about us than about God.

These problems of commercialization are real, though not fatal to CWM, and need to be addressed.

1. Does the process of composing, arranging, and producing CWM make it unsuitable for Christian worship?

---

gospel of grace. The prodigal son is "far away" from home when his father sights him; the tax collector stands "far away" when he prays in the temple — he is, after all, a tax collector (Luke 15 and 18).[39] So the apostles (the "ones who are sent") and their successors would go not only to Southern Europe, Northern Africa, and Western Asia, but everywhere in the world where people are "far away" from God. The idea, from Pentecost on, is to enable the peoples of the earth — the *whole* earth — to hear the word of the Lord and to ✗ render their thanks to God in a form suited to their own culture.

But why this great flurry of apostolic action to reach the peoples of the earth? What made this redemptive initiative so necessary?

39. Thomas G. Long, Calvin Institute for Christian Worship: Symposium on Worship and the Arts, Grand Rapids, Mich., 2001.

Among CWM companies, decisions about which songs to publish and record are made by relatively few people. To be sure, marketing considerations are a factor (will people like this?), but it is unfair to say that they are the only matters executives and producers bear in mind. Though most CWM labels accept little or no unsolicited material, they are not closed to anything new. Innovative material usually comes from composers known by executives and producers, although songs frequently used in corporate worship receive due notice as well. Only rarely does a song go onto a CD that is not "owned" by a congregation. So CWM companies generally see themselves as a conduit that passes music from the grassroots to a larger market, rather than as a creator that markets new music to consumers.

The creation of Christian Copyright Licensing, Inc., or CCLI, has solved many copyright woes for congregations. With this initiative, the CWM industry itself sought to help congregations, while also making their product easier to use legally.

Based on what we know of the production and publishing process, there is little here that makes a song unsuitable for Christian worship.

2. Does the process of marketing and distributing CWM make it unsuitable for worship?

Agreed, most CWM producers are for-profit companies, and in order to be more profitable they have made arrangements with larger music distribution companies and publishers, such as Chordant, Word, BMG, EMI, or Pamplin. This means CWM producers are less involved with mass marketing and distribution than they have been previously. At the same time, Internet commerce (e.g., www.worshipmusic.com) puts smaller companies

continued . . .

The biblical story in its broadest outline is the story of the creation, fall, redemption, and consummation of the whole earth and all its peoples. Pentecost fits into the redemptive phase of God's program, which had also included the covenant of grace with Abram (who then became "Abraham"), and the incarnation, ministry, death, and resurrection of Jesus Christ. Both the covenant of grace and the events of Jesus Christ had great social and cultural reach. The covenant with Abram and his people was meant to bless "all the families of the earth," and the work of Jesus Christ is meant to inspire "every knee [to] bend" and "every tongue [to] confess that Jesus Christ is Lord" (Gen. 12:3 and Phil. 2:10-11).

Each stage of the biblical drama shows us something about God's broad cultural interest, beginning with the story of creation in Gene-

and independent producers on the playing field alongside the distribution giants of the Big Three and CCM-affiliated labels. This can only benefit churches by making a wider variety of CWM easier to find and to acquire.

Unlike the production side of the CWM industry, the marketing and distributing side differs little from its secular counterpart. Sales are projected, tracked, and reported. Sales staff are always looking for new outlets, new customers, and new ways to get attention for their products. Designers create advertisements for magazines, in-store displays, and radio spots. Marketing staff look for ways to "tie-in" with their artist's live performances, or to connect with books by well-known Christian authors.

As mentioned, marketing and distributing decisions have not been as significant a factor in CWM producing and publishing decisions as they

have been in secular companies, and are likely to become even less important as distribution companies take the weight of marketing and advertising. Thus there should be little concern that the business of CWM in some way taints its product such that it is unsuitable for Christian worship.

∽

A more generous approach to commercial culture is possible. One may embrace commercial culture without affirming everything about it, particularly those aspects which conflict with biblical teaching. In his book *Selling God* (Oxford, 1994), Laurence Moore observes that "a sizeable portion of the Protestant evangelical community has made its peace with commercial culture by deciding to become a 'bigger road side attraction'" (p. 202). The tradition of evangelical entrepreneurialism carries on in a

---

sis 1. That story climaxes when God makes "humankind in our image, according to our likeness." Remarkably, the first order of business for these loftily designed creatures is to take a day off. The next is to develop human culture. In the so-called "cultural mandate," God charges humankind to be fruitful and multiply, to fill the earth and subdue it, to have dominion over the rest of creation (Gen. 1:28). Many theologians believe this mandate includes not only animal husbandry and earthkeeping but also marriage, family, language, commerce, and (even in an ideal world) government. The fall into sin corrupts these activities, but doesn't unlicense them. The same goes for the cultural initiatives of Genesis 4 — urban development, tent-making, musicianship, and metal-working. All of these are the unfolding of the built-in potential of God's good creation. All reflect

dynamic process by which commercial ventures both reflect and shape the worship of the evangelical subculture. Moore suggests that the either/or, "take it or leave it" extremism of some CWM critics fails to grant a nuanced view of commercial culture that invites Christians to engage that culture for the benefit of the church, which is surely the case with CWM.

The worship awakening owes much to the Christian worship music industry. For better or for worse, the commercial process will continue to be the primary means for distributing new worship music to churches. Pastors and worship leaders should be discerning consumers of its products, practicing the time-tested axiom "let the buyer beware."

Certainly the overabundance of CWM in recent years has created a feeling that many songs sound similar, or don't add anything to the range of wor-

ship themes. Seattle pastor Randy Rowland, whose church uses CWM almost exclusively, complained that praise and worship music seems to be stuck in a stylistic ghetto. "There is something disturbing about the Christian church, purportedly led by the Holy Spirit among whose characteristics one would assume would be creativity, whose art is mainly imitative. Where is the spiritual creativity in the midst of songs that all sound the same?" ("Stuck in a Musical Ghetto," *Worship Leader* 8, no. 5 [Sept./Oct. 1999]: 12).

Many worry about music production that resides in the hands of a relatively small group of artists, producers, and executives: shouldn't they be accountable to churches or denominations? Certainly a record company's "production values," the artistic decisions about repertoire and presentation, are often defined by the flow (and budget) of

continued . . .

---

some of the ingenuity of humankind, charged with working out some of the potential that God had worked into the creation. Even after the building trades had been corrupted for millennia — having been used to build Babel and Babylon, for example — Jesus adopted one of them as his own.

Sin damages God's creation, but doesn't destroy it. The result is that in the world as we actually know it — with all its opportunities for child-rearing, auto-racing, and empire-building — we will always find good and evil twined together in such a way that it takes a sharp eye to tell where the one leaves off and the other begins. Just as God approaches the world with both grace and judgment, so the child of God approaches culture with both a Yes and a No. The child of God is ready not only to receive the goodness of so much that God

the recording and marketing process, rather than by the needs of worshiping congregations. But these concerns can be overstated, and do not apply equally to all CWM producers. Vineyard Music Group/Mercy Publishing is a nonprofit venture completely accountable to Vineyard Ministries International, which, for all intents and purposes, is a denomination. Maranatha! Music and Integrity Music are for-profit corporations but include pastoral leadership on their board. Minor labels and CCM-sponsored projects vary in their relationship to churches. Some, like People of Destiny International, are operated by associations of churches, while others are subsidiaries of secular record companies. Churches often sponsor independent projects, the fastest-growing and most innovative source of CWM. Even denominations that at first were skeptical of CWM are now endorsing their own projects and resource guides.

In spite of this, it is clear that stronger links between CWM producers and users would be beneficial. CWM companies should welcome greater influence from the church. Together, churches and CWM companies can develop a fresh, theologically informed understanding of parachurch ministry. (The best place to start is Ray Anderson, *Minding God's Business* [Eerdmans, 1986].) A good model is the Vineyard Music Group, whose mission is to be an outlet for songwriters and worship leaders within the Vineyard Association of Churches, as well as a resource to the wider church. The company also partners with the Association in providing workshops for pastors, worship leaders, and team members. In similar ways, other record companies can invite theologians and pastors to gatherings of songwriters and producers to create dialogue and partnerships.

---

has bestowed and preserved by common grace but also to reject the serpents, within and without, that subvert God's purposes.

Reflecting on the original goodness of creation catapults our imaginations to the consummate goodness of the re-creation. There, too, we find both grace and judgment. Two of Scripture's dramatic visions of the new creation, the one chronicled by the prophet Isaiah and the other by the apostle John, tell us that the dignitaries of the earth will one day parade into the heavenly kingdom bearing their nation's glory with them (Isa. 60 and Rev. 21). These are dignitaries of every nation and tribe and language and people, and they lead the procession of a multitude so great it cannot be numbered. Isaiah pictures the treasures of his day being brought into the holy city — rams, camels, frankincense — but we can reframe the picture of the parade of nations. So the French will bring their Bordeaux wines, the Scots their tweeds, the Mayans their *xocoatl* (chocolate), the Chinese their Tang-dynasty vases, the Byzantines their mosaics, and the Liberians their woven bags. *But,* says John, nothing *unclean* will enter there (Rev. 21:27). There will be judgment. Dross will be consumed, and chaff will be sifted out.

What bearing should this vision have upon our engagement with culture, particularly when that engagement takes place for the sake of the gospel and the authentic worship of God?

CULTURAL ADAPTATION:
SEEKING THE WISDOM OF THE WORD MADE FLESH

So Pentecost, the creation, and the re-creation all offer insight into the relationship between worship and culture. But at the center of the biblical story we find another event that is often said to cast light on this relationship, namely, the incarnation.

The drafters of the 1996 "Nairobi Statement on Worship and Culture" assert that "in the mystery of [Jesus'] incarnation are the model and the mandate for the contextualization of Christian worship."[40] Jesus was born into a specific culture of the world, and his life assumed that cultural context. Accordingly, our worship, too, should be "born into" and "assume" its cultural context, though only insofar as the values and patterns of culture are "consonant with the values of the Gospel."[41]

Along lines now familiar to us, the Nairobi Statement acknowledges the need for both grace and judgment. Other paragraphs reinforce the judgment part of the summons, first by appealing to Paul's letter to the Romans where he urges believers, "Do not be

---

40. "Nairobi Statement on Worship and Culture," paragraph 3.1, as found in *Christian Worship: Unity in Cultural Diversity,* ed. S. Anita Stauffer (Geneva: The Lutheran World Federation, 1996), p. 25.

41. "Nairobi Statement," paragraph 3.1, p. 25.

conformed to this world"; and then by appealing to Christ's death and resurrection. But the Statement finds in Christ's incarnation itself more of a model for acculturation in worship than for critique of culture.[42]

The same goes for Tex Sample. With respect to the incarnation and its implications for worship, Sample follows much the same line of reasoning as the Nairobi Statement, but ups the ante where acculturation is concerned by recommending aggressive forms of it. Pointing out that "the Word became flesh and 'pitched tent' *with us*,"[43] Sample suggests that worship should do the same. Worship should "become flesh" and "pitch tent" with the accoutrements of contemporary culture so that it will become a crowd-grabbing, attention-holding "spectacle" not unlike a Michael Jackson concert or the opening ceremonies of the Olympics.[44]

What makes these events "spectacles"? The choreography of lights and sound, staging and screening, which is exactly the luster Sample wants to see in Christian worship. To Sample, worship that fails to "become flesh" and "pitch tent" in the accoutrements of contemporary culture fails to be "Incarnational."[45] It fails to engage with culture in a way that is "basic to the Christian faith."[46]

In his very next sentence, Sample admits a word of caution: there are some practices that are "clearly in violation of the faith."[47] But his only example (orgies) is so far outside Christian practice that his word of caution lacks traction. What about a Christian musician who strolls into the church's spotlight and expresses her love for Jesus with all the practiced moves and vocal inflections of a lounge singer? What about singing the coda of Whitney Houston's 1992 hit from *The Bodyguard,* "I Will Always Love You," as a response to Christ's call to discipleship? What

---

42. "Nairobi Statement," paragraph 4.1, p. 27.
43. Sample, *Spectacle of Worship,* p. 105. Emphasis Sample's.
44. Sample, *Spectacle of Worship,* pp. 56f.
45. Sample, *Spectacle of Worship,* pp. 105, 106.
46. Sample, *Spectacle of Worship,* p. 106.
47. Sample, *Spectacle of Worship,* p. 106.

about dressing up the ministry staff with Santa hats and ties for Christmas morning worship?

Sample does understand that items from popular culture need to be shaped to fit into Christian worship. He moreover believes that reworking these items amounts to an implicit cultural critique. But all the reworking or redefining of popular culture is to happen *in* worship *for* worship. Cultural critique is to take place simultaneously *with* worship. Such a method raises questions: Just how much accommodation of culture is fitting for worship? And just how clear is the critique, especially for those whose tools for sizing it up — namely, Scripture and faith — are hardly broken in? Put theologically, the question is whether accommodation to the world is explicit in Jesus' incarnation and judgment of the world only implicit.

One more observer of the meaning of the incarnation for Christian worship: In his book *Out on the Edge,* Michael Slaughter suggests that the incarnation is primarily a means for God to let us get to know him. It's an opportunity for us to "grasp the infinite God," to experience God's glory on a "multi-sensory level."[48] Jesus' ministry, it seems, was something of a marketing campaign, and the church should follow suit, using "the wisdom of the world" as its means for serving God.[49] Of course, by adopting the wisdom of the world, including the trappings of secular culture, innovators in the church can expect to take some heat, just as Jesus did from the Pharisees and from John the Baptist's disciples. According to Slaughter, Jesus' critics thought he was "too comfortable with people on the outside. He was too much fun to be spiritual! Jesus was not separate from sinners. He was a friend of sinners. A friend who knew how to have a good time!"[50] So a good time, it seems, is just what we must have in worshiping God.

Once again, questions arise. Suppose we agree with Slaughter

---

48. Slaughter, *Out on the Edge,* p. 43.
49. Slaughter, *Out on the Edge,* pp. 36ff., 44ff., especially 47-48.
50. Slaughter, *Out on the Edge,* p. 47.

that all truth is God's truth. Does the same go for all of culture? If everything God has created is good, does the same go for everything humans have produced since then?

Presumably not. If the Son of God became the One through whom "God was pleased to reconcile to himself all things" (Col. 1:20), maybe the reason for this program is that all those "things" had become divided and otherwise corrupt. If so, popular forms of entertainment are not exempt. "Do not be conformed to the world" applies to the world of entertainment too.

It doesn't follow that Christians should detach from culture. In fact, Christians have been called to take a part in God's reconciliation and reformation of all things. But here lies a famous old problem. If Christians fail to engage the world of secular culture in order to protect themselves from its temptations, they cannot live and witness in the real world. They can't even understand it. They can't address unbelievers in a language unbelievers understand. But if Christians get close enough to secular culture to understand it, to witness to it, to try in some ways to reform it — or even to use it in the worship of God — how will Christians keep from being seduced by the worldliness within this culture, and how will they keep from polluting their worship of God?

The point is that the redemption of culture with reference to Christian worship is a difficult project, requiring mighty thought and prayer. It won't be enough to approach worship with the hope of having a good time. It won't be enough to hope that we can redeem forms of popular culture simply by using them to worship God. Israel's golden calf was still an idol, even when it became part of "a festival to the Lord" (Exod. 32:5), and the children of Israel did not necessarily understand the use of the calf as an implied critique of idolatry.

Christ's incarnation is often invoked as a precedent for the "incarnation" of our worship in contemporary culture, and it's a natural move: Jesus engaged his culture and we should engage ours. Jesus was "born into" a particular culture, and so our worship should be "born into" ours. This line of thinking is straight so far as it goes.

But it falls short, so it seems to us, of a fuller understanding of the meaning of the incarnation, and in three ways. First, it's much too simple to suppose that the point of the incarnation was for God to get close to us. Scripture answers the question "Why did God become human?" in a number of ways. Christ came "to destroy the works of the devil" (1 John 3:8). He came "to deal with sin" and to fulfill the Law (Rom. 8:3-4). He came "to seek out and to save the lost" (Luke 19:10). In his longest reach, he came "to gather up all things," or "to reconcile all things" to God (Eph. 1:10; Col. 1:20). The Scriptures use a riot of terms and images to describe the force of Jesus' work, but one way or another they all say that Jesus Christ came to put right what we human beings had put wrong by our sin. Thus, he came in order to be "the atoning sacrifice for our sins" (1 John 4:10) and "to give his life a ransom for many" (Mark 10:45). Perhaps we may see here that "accessibility" and "visibility" don't rise to the top of scriptural reasons for the incarnation, and that emphasis upon them for a theology of worship is therefore bound to be scripturally marginal.

Second, even if Jesus was "a friend of sinners," it wouldn't follow that a primary purpose of the incarnation was God's wish to become our best buddy. Throughout Scripture, the people of God are instructed to "fear" the Lord, to revere and honor, to love and obey the Lord. This fear, of course, isn't what the angel of the Lord meant to dispel after he startled the one whom he had come to visit. "Do not be afraid!" is a word of grace, meant to reassure the terrified. But once this is done, God doesn't then become a chum. Just because Christ relinquished his crown for a time doesn't mean that he became any less God — or that he made God any less. Through Christ we have access to the Father (Eph. 2:18), but it doesn't follow that God may be casually addressed. Christ laid down his life for his friends, but he remains their Lord. Indeed, for the climax of his incarnate mission, one day "every knee should bend, in heaven and on earth and under the earth, and every tongue should confess that Jesus Christ is Lord, to the glory of God the Father" (Phil. 2:10-11).

Third, the incarnation brings with it not only God's grace but also

Two Sketches from a Parish Choir Room
Ted A. Gibboney

Music is a matter of the heart. Our experience with music conveys something about not just our preferences but also our identity.

I

It was a hot summer afternoon when the phone rang in my office. The voice on the other end was that of a nurse attending one parishioner of the suburban Presbyterian church I was serving at the time. The parishioner, Alice, was recovering from a minor surgery that took place in her final months of gradual decline due to Alzheimer's disease. She was regaining consciousness slowly and it was only with difficulty that the nurse could communicate with her.

As the nurse sat at Alice's bedside, she discovered that Alice would respond when she sang to her. So the nurse sang favorite gospel hymns and spirituals from her African-American tradition. Since Alice responded positively to the music, the nurse thought it would be a good idea to find a recording of such music, which was the reason she called for my help. It was with some reluctance that I went to the church library and obtained the 1975 Baptist hymnal and prepared the recording equipment in the church choir room.

Two striking things occurred because of that informal tape recording. First, as I played through the Baptist hymnal, my thoughts were transported back to my childhood. During my grandmother's last years she often asked me to play some of those same gospel hymns for her. Even now I can hear her gravelly voice enthusiastically droning somewhere in the vicinity of my playing.

God's judgment, and any theology of worship that appeals to the incarnation must take both into account. To be sure, Christ became *human,* the son of a blue-collar tradesman of the tribe of Judah. As Christians we readily acknowledge not just that Christ became human, but that he became *fully* human. By such a confession we mean to assert that all that Christ became, Christ redeemed; and since Christ became flesh, we may be assured that he redeems flesh, and that he will one day redeem *our* flesh. But the point of such a profession is not that Christ's incarnation somehow validates all of human existence, including culture. Obivously not. Sin corrupts human existence, including culture, and corruption is what Christ came to defeat. If God made "him to be sin who knew no sin" (2 Cor. 5:21), God did not do

Second, the tape recording produced the desired effect. Alice recovered from her surgery, and during the last months of her life played that recording. During the last days of her life, at a time when the names of her husband and children were indistinct, she remembered the names of members of her choir, her church, and her Christian community because of that tape.

II

During the fall of 1987 I began as Minister of Music for the First Baptist Church of Indianapolis. A group of youth and adult leaders had just returned from the international conference of the Baptist World Alliance, which had been held in Edinburgh, Scotland, the previous summer. Their lives were changed by the experience of getting to know youth from around the world and worshiping with

them at mass rallies. The students bought one of the hymnals that was a primary resource for that event: *Let's Praise* (Marshall Pickering, 1988, available from Hope Publishing). An outgrowth of the youth rally movement in England and Scotland, this hymnal includes songs such as "Bind Us Together" and "Shine, Jesus, Shine."

One of the leaders of that group was named David. He was a husband, a father of nine, a successful businessman, and an active, beloved leader in the church. Tragedy struck. As the result of a bad business deal, a contract was put out on David's life. He was shot and killed late one night near his business. The horror of the act stunned the family, our congregation, and our community. Our grief was intense, and shared. The local media coverage in newspapers and on radio and television added to the surreal and unforgettable impressions of the funeral.

continued . . .

---

so to recommend sin but to absorb it into himself, to atone for it, to (one day) rid the world of it.

So in Christ's very incarnation we find both grace and judgment. There is grace in that Christ "emptied himself, taking the form of a slave, being born in human likeness" (Phil. 2:7); but there is also judgment, in that this human likeness "came to destroy the works of the devil" (1 John 3:8).

Grace and judgment are marks of Jesus' ministry, too. In Martin Luther King Jr.'s terms, we might say that Christ was "maladjusted" to human existence, rather than "adjusted" to it. Believing the hope of humanity lay in the hands of the "creatively maladjusted," King once professed,

It is not surprising that the songs on the lips of those youth are indelibly ingrained in their minds because of experiences. When they returned from Scotland, they sang "Bind Us Together" and "Shine, Jesus, Shine" with joyful and youthful exuberance. "Shine, Jesus, Shine" was chosen for David's funeral because of the way it reflected his personality, and our own need to cling to Christ at a time of intense grief. It was the youth who requested that "Shine, Jesus, Shine" be a part of the following Easter services, as we nurtured our faith in another life, and our love and memories of those sad experiences.

∼

In situations like these, theological and aesthetic responses fall short of the call. A pastoral response is called for too.

Often we approach examples like these from one of two simplistic points of view. The first, concerned with "truth," marshals all the resources of theology and aesthetics to critique. The second, concerned with "grace," scoffs at these potentially heartless critiques, and seeks to minister with the music people love.

But what would it look like to minister with a concern for both grace and truth? What would it mean to take seriously the important, soul-shaping experiences people have with music, and the significant insights that come from unapologetically deep reflection on Scripture and theological tradition?

There are some things in our social order to which I am proud to be maladjusted and to which I call upon you to be maladjusted. I never intend to adjust myself to segregation and discrimination. I never intend to adjust myself to mob rule. I never intend to adjust myself to the tragic effects of the methods of physical violence.[51]

Christ was never particularly "adjusted" either. He worshiped in the temple, but he also cleansed it. He called one tax collector to be his disciple, but he also chided the embezzling practices that went along with this civic office. He healed and forgave, but he also invited those healed and forgiven to "go and sin no more."

Mercy *entails* judgment. Sick people need healing, but first they need a diagnosis. Sinners need forgiveness, but first they need to

---

51. Martin Luther King Jr., "The Power of Nonviolence," in *A Testament of Hope: The Essential Writings of Martin Luther King, Jr.*, ed. James Melvin Washington (San Francisco: Harper and Row, 1986), p. 14.

know their sin. Like a diagnosis, God's judgment brings pain, but it also brings hope. Something can be done about sin — in fact, something *has* been done about it. So the forgiven sinner is invited into the glorious liberty of the children of God, a condition of enormous joy and satisfaction. But none of this is possible without judgment.

It's the same with Christ's crucifixion. His sentence is our acquittal. When Scripture speaks of the incarnation, the themes of salvation, redemption, and reconciliation — won for us by the cross of Christ — are never far away. It's in the incarnate Word, crucified on the cross, that we find the ultimate manifestation of both God's Yes! and God's No! — God's gracious covenant and God's righteous judgment upon the whole of humanity.[52]

So rather than settling our dilemma over the contextualization or the *in*culturation of worship, the incarnation actually sharpens it. While it's desirable to clothe worship in cultural attire, ultimately the incarnation invites us to be tailors with an eye for what fits. In every dimension of the incarnation we find both grace and judgment, which isn't so much a clashing combination as a creatively matched one. Grace and judgment exist together, and they're exercised together, the one within the context of the other.

CULTURAL ADAPTATION: IT'S "MESSY"

Managing the tension between judgment and grace requires discernment, no less in the cultural adaptation of worship than in the rest of life lived "in the world but not of it." What we're looking for here is the fitting *adaptation* of worship to culture. What we want is to make worship the object of adaptation, with culture as its context, rather than making culture the object of adaptation, with worship as its context. Worship should be culturally connected not for the sake of culture but for the sake of worship. First things first.

52. Karl Barth, *Evangelical Theology: An Introduction* (Grand Rapids: Eerdmans, 1963), pp. 78-79.

Exactly how the adaptation of worship goes will depend in part upon our approach to culture. Do we believe it warrants more judgment than grace, or more grace than judgment? Are we suspicious of its worth, or enthusiastic? Given the illustrations at the beginning of this chapter, what will be our response? Some of those scenarios demand tough calls, tougher than we might like to admit, whether our overall reaction is acceptance or rejection. As Gordon Lathrop has suggested, when it comes to deciding what in culture is to be accepted and what is to be rejected, there is no neat, authoritarian answer, but only a "messy" one.[53] Finding it requires humility.

So some parts of the worldwide church will say No — no to things like Super Bowl extravaganzas, aggressive rock music, and casual preaching. In their pastoral judgment, these are accommodations to culture that breach the integrity of worship. They send messages — about the roles of men and women, the commercial market, and the integrity of our speech — that cross the gospel's message. But then other parts of the worldwide church will say Yes — yes to things like folk music, drama troupes, and prayers of lament inspired by newspaper headlines. In their pastoral judgment, these nuances are a legitimate contextualization of worship.

In most cases, attempts at cultural adaptation will have a "both/and" feel to them. They will exhibit both grace and judgment. Churches will do as God did when creating the sea: they will mark a line in the sand and say, "This far you may go, and no farther" (cf. Jer. 5:22). So one church will add a praise band, but will also set a standard for its repertoire. Another church may welcome a less formal preaching style, but also call for sermons that are more rigorously expository. Still another congregation may incorporate drama, provided most presentations are straight renditions of biblical texts.

Fortunately, we don't make such calls about cultural adaptation alone, not even the really tough ones. Discernment is a gift of the Spirit given not to individuals but to a community, and the com-

---

53. Gordon Lathrop, "Worship: Local Yet Universal," in *Christian Worship: Unity in Cultural Diversity* (Geneva: Lutheran World Federation, 1996).

munity to which it's given includes people from around the world throughout all of history. For nearly two millennia now, that community — namely, the church — has been interpreting not only Scripture but also Christian worship itself, and its backlog of wisdom is ours to plumb. Jean Bethke Elshtain once lamented that contemporary culture seems to assume that "our ancestors knew less than we."[54] C. S. Lewis called this "chronological snobbery."[55] No matter what we call it, it's lamentable because of the way it disenfranchises members of the church, which transcends time.

> *"Tradition means giving votes to the most obscure of all classes — our ancestors. It . . . refuses to submit to the small and arrogant oligarchy of those who merely happen to be walking around."*
>
> G. K. Chesterton, *Orthodoxy* (New York: Lane, 1909), p. 85

When it comes to "contextualizing the faith," says Max Stackhouse, we are not alone. We are, in fact, "in the company of the saints of the past" even as we "turn to the future."[56] Perhaps, says Stackhouse, we should think of our position in this way: "we are still in the age of contextualizing the faith, an age which extends from Pentecost to the eschaton, and a faith that is relevant to every particular context."[57] That is, with respect to the gospel and to worship, our context is both an age that spans history and a faith that spans the globe. If that's the case, concludes Stackhouse, then "Wesley had it right when he said, 'the world is my parish,' and Troeltsch had it right when he wrote 'history is our epoch.'"[58] That's the breadth of our context because that's the breadth of our community.

While the nature of this community, which is the church, will be explored in greater depth in the next chapter, we might notice now that this community is a co-culture. In fact, it's a co-culture that it-

54. Jean Bethke Elshtain, "Ethics, Education, and Civic Life," *The January Series,* Calvin College, Grand Rapids, Mich., 14 January 1993.

55. C. S. Lewis, *Surprised by Joy* (New York: Harcourt, Brace, © 1956 by C. S. Lewis and renewed 1984 by Arthur Owen Barfield), p. 207.

56. Max L. Stackhouse, "Contextualization, Contextuality, and Contextualism," in *One Faith, Many Cultures: Inculturation, Indigenization, and Contextualization,* ed. Ruy O. Costa (Maryknoll, N.Y.: Orbis, 1988), p. 5.

57. Stackhouse, "Contextualization," p. 12.

58. Stackhouse, "Contextualization," p. 13.

self comprises a number of cultures. Recalling Samovar and Porter's definition we're reminded that a co-culture is a people group that exists within a society but outside the dominant culture.[59] Being resident aliens, strangers in a strange land, in the world but not of it, members of the church make up just such a people group. While the church must engage mainstream culture, its identity runs somewhere alongside it. This is part of our "creative maladjustment," as Martin Luther King Jr. might call it.

Earlier in this chapter, we said that the cultural adaptation of worship is desirable, in part because it removes any "unnecessary obstacles" to a newcomer's participation in the life of the church. This is well and good: hospitality ought to be a prominent feature of Christian worship. But, as we also suggested earlier, the question remains whether there are any "necessary obstacles" that the church ought to preserve.

Like the co-cultures Samovar and Porter identify to illustrate their point, the church has its own patterns of speech and practice. We confess our sins, and preach the word of God, and celebrate the sacraments. We sing, and pray, and recite our beliefs. In whatever cultural milieu they are given expression, accompanied by hula hand gestures or conga drums or Genevan psalm tunes, these elements might be considered "necessary obstacles" in our worship. These are things for which the church should not apologize. They are, after all, part of the church's shared memory, part of its identity and distinction. They are part of the church's way of passing on faith and preserving faith's integrity within the worship of its community.

Exactly *how* they are taken up is, again, a matter of discernment, but neither the longtime churchgoer nor the newcomer should be shy about the fact *that* these practices are taken up. Instead, each should foster a mutual respect for the other. Hospitality is a two-way street — the host must be a good host, and the guest must be a good

---

59. Samovar and Porter, *Communication between Cultures*, p. 158.

guest. Being a good host means graciously presenting a practice, and being a good guest means graciously observing it. As their life of faith matures, aided by the church's habits of piety, newcomers may come to have a deeper understanding of these practices, perhaps, in due course, deeper than that of many life-long members.

Chapter 4

The Bond of Peace:
The Worshiping *Church*

"UNITY IN DIVERSITY" HAS BECOME SOMETHING of a catchphrase these days. Log onto the Internet, Google, for "unity in diversity," and the top ten of more than forty-one thousand hits will appear in less than a second. And who's staking a claim with this phrase? A quick scan of the search results will tell you that they're especially university professionals, Baha'i spiritualists, and Whirlpool executives. In nearly every case, institutions employ this phrase in their attempt to deal with the fact of "diversity" in North America.

Stand before an ATM and the first thing it wants to know is whether you wish to do business in English or in Spanish. Walk the aisles of an urban supermarket and listen to three or four different languages — and that's not counting the mall-speak of the two teens stocking shelves. Yankee English is scripted for the anchors of CNN Headline News, though hundreds of dialects are spoken among its viewers in homes, med center waiting rooms, and airport terminals all over the country. In some communities in North America, three services of worship may be held in a single building in a given week, each service conducted in a different language. Immigrants have crossed North America's borders for centuries, and the complexion of every community reflects this in some way.

In many discussions about North America's ethnic multiplicity, the phrase "unity in diversity" is supplemented with the term "multiculturalism." Like "unity in diversity," "multiculturalism" is a term coined only within the last several decades, and it's immediately ambiguous. In an essay entitled "All Quiet on the (Post) Western Front?" Clifford Orwin (with thanks to his colleague H. D. Forbes) notes a difference between multiculturalism as a fact and multiculturalism as a policy.[1] As a fact, multiculturalism simply refers to the reality with which many of us are familiar, the reality that we called to mind above. As noted in the previous chapter, North American society is a culture of cultures, a tapestry of nations that piques delight. That's multiculturalism celebrated as a fact. But then there's multiculturalism employed as a policy to answer questions raised by multiculturalism as a fact: How do we integrate students or employees, or clients or customers, of various cultural backgrounds? How do we recognize the integrity and shore up the dignity of each particular kind of person?

As a policy, multiculturalism began with an impulse toward hospitality — the same impulse that inspires a call to "unity in diversity." Sad to say, in many cases that healthy impulse has now hardened into an ideology, just as an "-ism" implies. If granted ideological status, then multiculturalism can mean that every culture, along with every cultural practice, must be validated — not judged, but validated; not assessed, but appreciated. Truth is relative to persons and to cultures, with the result that what may be "true for you" is not necessarily "true for me." Ideas can be neither tested nor contested; they can only be shared. Standards for assessing good and bad, right and wrong, moral and immoral are culture-specific and assumed to be beyond reproach. Openness to their legitimacy is mandatory, and the person who demurs becomes guilty of the sin of intolerance.

1. Clifford Orwin, "All Quiet on the (Post) Western Front?" *The Public Interest* 123 (Spring 1996): 3-21.

What sometimes accompanies such ideological relativism is a "politics of identity" that tends to balkanize the co-cultures that make up a single society. Such politics corrupts unity even as it salutes diversity. Groups — or co-cultures — are labeled, becoming the pigeonholes in which individual folk are supposed to live. Then these pigeonholes proliferate, so that we have not just, say, an auto workers' union, but a black auto workers' union, and then a Romanian auto workers' union and a women's auto workers' union, and then an auto workers' union for women of African and Romanian descent. The point is that a single characteristic of one's persona (or maybe a particular combination of two or three or four characteristics) will become one's personal ID.

Often the marketplace helps define the labels on our ID. Niche marketing, of everything from automobiles to Bibles to fashion accessories, powerfully influences the balkanization of North American culture. In 2001, the Bollé eyewear company, noted for its cutting-edge, sport-specific sunglasses, ran a print ad that featured a shark-bitten surfboard, two or three items of bloody swimwear afloat nearby, and an intact pair of Bollé sunglasses perched jauntily on a surviving piece of the surfboard. The caption? "Bollé: Tougher than you are."

"Now if selves are defined by their preferences, but those preferences are arbitrary, then each self constitutes its own moral universe, and there is finally no way to reconcile conflicting claims about what is good in itself. All we can do is to refer to chains of consequences and ask if our actions prove useful or consistent in light of our own 'value systems.' All we can appeal to in relationships with others is their self-interest, likewise enlightened, or their intuitive sympathies."

From *Habits of the Heart*, by Robert Bellah et al. (Berkeley: University of California Press, 1985), p. 76

Work, age, gender, ethnic or national origin, economic status, *machismo* in the right sunglasses — these and many other identifiers combine to provide North Americans with their ID card. The card is useful not only to advertisers but also to anybody who wants "a place at the table" when it comes to deciding equitable arrangements in a diverse culture. At this table (think of a public school board meeting) dialogue carries on among equals. According to proper political etiquette, we set up our roundtables *at round tables,* where there is neither head nor foot. Equal truths get equal time. No thought is a trivial thought. Each person's contribution is recognized. But because participants can't really debate issues according to a shared understanding of truth (that impossibility is itself undebatable), consensus is more of an accident than an achievement. All depends on who happens to be at the table that day. Worse, if participants care passionately about what's being discussed, and lack a shared standard for debate, their dialogue may degenerate into a clash of opinions or, worse, a power struggle. No more polite recognition of everybody's right to a place at the table. Now the idea is winning. So participants make and break alliances, form parties, trade favors — whatever it takes to prevail.

In many contemporary North American settings, "unity in diversity" turns out to be a troubled phenomenon. Power struggles don't look much like unity, but neither does the "live and let live" philosophy of equal recognition. If "no thought is a trivial thought," all we have at the end of the day is a mound of unsorted contributions. Everybody has been recognized, but it's hard to say that anything like *unity* has been achieved.

Unfortunately, the politics of identity appears not just within the ivory towers of academe or the marble halls of government. It also shows up within the Christian church, on a global, a national, and a congregational level. For now let's look at the last.

What about the Church?

Once upon a time, church members glared at each other over doctrinal disputes — even small ones, as it seems in retrospect. But in today's balkanized environment, disputes might be about anything, from how big the pastor's office should be to whom the church should ordain; from the color of the carpet in the sanctuary to, of course, how people ought to worship there.

Remarkably, Christians quarrel with each other over the question of how to adore God. Church officers sometimes try to prevent the quarrels with a roundtable strategy of equal recognition of all. "We're keeping everybody happy," they say. "Different strokes for different folks," they say, "so let's try to blend those strokes and keep our folks."

As with secular culture, so with the church: niche marketing tends to reinforce our differences — in fact, to highlight them. Worship planners specifically target three or four identity groupings in their own church, and worship planning resources come with predefined audiences in mind. With apparently nothing to learn from others, the planning resources appear to start from scratch to fill their audience niche — perhaps generating a sophisticated publishing company, a web-ring, and a year-round conference schedule, all aimed at a particular market segment of the church.

It's not that marketing itself is a problem: it's the way marketing is done, and how it is received. As often happens, even good ideas (Let's keep everybody happy) can generate unhappy consequences, such as a "party spirit" within the church. "Party spirit" in the Christian church has little to do with having a good time. It has everything to do with the clashing of special interests, or even of factions. For example:

• *Attend a conference on worship and church music and you're sure to hear at least one beleaguered minister or music director tell a story that begins something like this:*

> *Once a month I receive a note in my mailbox from a member of my congregation. The note is a tally of the songs that were sung in church, a complex box score according to musical style and instrumental accompaniment. The score might be fifteen to fourteen in favor of . . . , and this person will complain that last month. . . .*

- *Worship leaders make an off-hand comment that dismisses other brothers and sisters in Christ: "I'll bet they don't have this much fun at the Episcopal church!" And maybe the Episcopal church returns the favor: "No dumbed-down worship here!"*

- *A church solves its problems by simply adding another service. Its newspaper ad reads, "See that the Lord is good, no matter what your taste," after which several services are listed: On Sunday mornings, traditional worship at 8:30, contemporary at 10:00, and charismatic at 11:30. On Saturday evenings at 6:00 and 8:00, praise with a postmodern pulse.*

- *A church's one service of worship is earnestly eclectic — or, more softly termed, "blended" — with each interest group granted a weekly or monthly quota.*

- *Communication goes awry, if it exists at all. Worship leaders, such as a guitarist and an organist, never speak to one another, never cross-fertilize their worship planning and music-making.*

- *Intimidation tactics may be employed: Some youth inquire about having their band lead worship one Sunday evening, to which the minister of music replies, "Over my dead body!" Or, super-charged by a conference on contemporary worship, a minister appropriates the choir director's budget for music and new robes in favor of PowerPoint software and an Epson PowerLite multi-media projector.*

- *The minister and worship planning team assume that criticism of their "newfangled service" is a sign that they are following the way of Christ: Didn't Christ suffer criticism from the Pharisees for his newfangled teaching?*

"Party spirit" in the church, as we have said, is caused by the clashing of special interests. In the attempt to mollify the various parties, church leaders cater to them. But this move, though understandable, imports into the church a troubled ideology of contemporary secularism. The sad result is a local communion that professes to be "one," but whose everyday reality is more like a small group of factions in uneasy cohabitation. They may say "Peace, peace" when there is no peace, but only a façade for their strife. Enthusiasts of the policy of "equal time for equal interests" or "we have ours here, and you have yours there" may say, "See? Unity . . . in diversity!" But all there is to see is diversity. To the maximum degree possible, each interest group in the church is granted its wish, and so we have diversity, almost a kaleidoscope; but where is the unity?

To gain traction in thinking about diversity and unity in the Christian church, we'll have to look outside secular ideologies. Christians have their own way of thinking about unity and diversity. The way Christians think about this phenomenon comes from the center of their faith, which in turn influences what they think about the church and how they fashion their worship.

UNION WITH CHRIST

To be a Christian is to be united with Jesus Christ. According to Scripture, the death and resurrection of Christ are "for us," "for many," "for all" (Rom. 5:8, 15, 18). He was "handed over to death for our trespasses and was raised for our justification" (Rom. 4:25). The problem, as John Calvin wrote, is that "as long as Christ remains outside of us . . . all that he has suffered and done for the salvation of the human race remains useless . . . ; all that he possesses is nothing to us until we grow into one body with him."[2]

"Until we grow into one body with him." Calvin is talking about our union with Christ, by the Holy Spirit, and, in the same breath, about the Christian church. What Calvin knew is that Jesus Christ did not rise alone. He was raised as the head of a whole body of people chosen to have faith in him, to benefit from him, and to extend his

2. John Calvin, *Institutes of the Christian Religion*, 2 vols., ed. John T. McNeill, trans. Ford Lewis Battles (Philadelphia: Westminster, 1960), 1:537 (3.1.1).

mission in the world (Rom. 11:5-6; Eph. 1:4; 2 Thess. 2:13). Believers unite with Christ through "the secret energy of the Holy Spirit"[3] and through faith, and believers express this faith and absorb this energy through whole-hearted participation in the church and her means of grace. "To be 'saved,'" says Gordon Fee, "means especially to be joined to the people of God . . . because God is saving *a people* for his name, not a miscellaneous, unconnected set of individuals."[4] In New Testament thinking, nobody gains union with Christ by himself; no one is in Christ by herself. We are never free agents. As Christians we are members of a worldwide and a local body, a whole team of believers, a "great cloud of witnesses" (Heb. 12:1).

In a commentary on his catechism, one minister of the Reformation wrote that "when anyone prays alone in his closet, the whole church prays with him in affection and desire."[5] And so, appropriately, the classic events by which a person attaches to Jesus Christ are corporate. The preaching of the gospel is a corporate event. Baptism and the Lord's Supper are *church* sacraments, intended to bind to Christ and to each other a whole body of people who don't necessarily even like each other very well. Some are originally Jews; others Greeks. Some lean left in their politics; others right. Some want pipe organs; others, guitar amps. Some want a projection screen; others, hymnbooks. Like spokes, the only place these folks fit together is at their hub. Somehow they must all fit "into" Christ. This can be accomplished only by, in, and through the Holy Spirit. As Lewis Smedes once put it, "the Spirit is the living contact between the victorious Jesus and all who are united with Him."[6]

It follows, then, that these folk must fit into God. This dangerous-sounding claim means no more (and no less) than what Jesus

---

3. Calvin, *Institutes*, 1:537 (3.1.1).

4. Gordon Fee, *Paul, the Spirit, and the People of God* (Peabody, Mass.: Hendrickson, 1996), p. 64. Emphasis Fee's. See also the preface of the same work, p. ix.

5. Zacharius Ursinus, *The Commentary of Dr. Zacharius Ursinus on the Heidelberg Catechism*, trans. G. W. Williard (Grand Rapids: Eerdmans, 1954), p. 628.

6. Lewis B. Smedes, *Union with Christ: A Biblical View of the New Life in Jesus Christ* (Grand Rapids: Eerdmans, 1983), p. 26.

meant when he prayed, "As you, Father, are in me, and I am in you, may they also be in us . . ." (John 17:21). Christians function with a common identity and mission not only because they belong to the body of Christ, but also because Christ's body, the church, is an emblem of the Holy Trinity. This is so because Christ himself is a complementary member of a "body," or a society. Christians believe not only in Jesus Christ but also in the triune God, of whom Christ is the incarnate second person. Together, the doctrines of Christ and of the Holy Trinity give Christians a special way to think about unity within diversity.

UNITY AND DIVERSITY IN TRINITARIAN PERSPECTIVE

"The Father is God, the Son is God, and the Holy Spirit is God," says the Athanasian Creed, "and yet . . . there is only one God." "The Father is eternal, the Son is eternal, and the Holy Spirit is eternal, and yet . . . there is but one eternal being." In the Creed, God is a balanced, symmetrical triad of perfectly mirrored equalities. "Nothing in this trinity is before or after; nothing is greater or smaller."

The creed smooths out the biblical portrait of the divine persons in ways that needn't detain us here. And yet, with good reason Christians believe that these three — in their interlocking relationships — may properly be named and worshiped as one God. As the Creed says, we "worship their trinity in their unity and their unity in their trinity." In fact, the *koinonia* inside the divine life is what Jesus pointed to as a model for the unity of distinct persons within the Christian church.

In reflecting on this model, St. Augustine wrote that the persons of the Holy Trinity were perfectly one in essence, and perfectly united in their work. Because of their mutual interrelation, the work of one person is the work of all three. None of the divine persons is an independent contractor.

Yet each is distinct, and the distinctions within God were not lost on so great a defender of "one God" as Augustine. Very near the beginning of all his hard thinking on the Trinity, Augustine notes that it was the Son who was begotten and the Father who did the begetting, and that the Spirit is neither begotten nor begets (is neither the Son nor the Father), but is still God. It wasn't the Trinity that spoke from a cloud saying, "This is my Son," but the Father. It wasn't the Trinity that descended upon Jesus in the Jordan nor later upon the apostles at Pentecost, but the Spirit. It wasn't the Trinity that was crucified, died, and was buried, but the Son.[7]

So what permits us to say "one God"? Where's the unity?

Following Augustine and other thinkers in the history of the church, we note that the writers of Scripture sometimes use "one God" to designate God the Father, as Paul does in 1 Corinthians 8: 6 ("yet for us there is one God, the Father, . . . and one Lord, Jesus Christ"). But to understand the oneness of the church we need to turn back to the Fourth Gospel. "I and the Father are one," says Jesus in John 10:30.

One what? One father? One person?

Neither.

Throughout John's Gospel, Father and Son (and, sometimes, Spirit) have one word (3:34; 14:26). They also have one will (10:18) and one work (5:19; 16:14). They further know, love, and glory in each other (10:15, 17; 16:14; 17:24). All this is summed up in the climactic seventeenth chapter where Jesus prays to the Father for those who will believe because of the witness of the disciples:

> I ask not only on behalf of these, but also on behalf of those who will believe in me through their word, that they may all be one. As you, Father, are in me and I am in you, may they also be in us. . . . The glory that you have given me I have given them, so that they may be one, as we are one. (17:20-22)

7. Augustine, *On the Trinity*, vol. 1 of *The Works of Saint Augustine: A Translation for the Twenty-First Century*, ed. John E. Rotelle, intro., trans., and notes by Edmund P. Hill (Brooklyn, N.Y.: New City Press, 1991, 2000), p. 69 (1.2.7).

How are Father and Son (and Paraclete) one? In word, and work, and will. In knowledge, love, and glory. That is, in action and in essence. An implication is that each belongs to the other two. The Father, Son, and Spirit are all "members one of another" to a superlative degree. The Father and the Son are begetter and begotten. The Son is, so to speak, "his Father all over again." And the Spirit is "the Spirit of the Father"; "the Spirit of the Son"; "the Spirit of God." The Holy Trinity is not a set of three miscellaneous divine persons who decide to join forces, for none can be God without the other two. And their titles suggest that they are not just members of the same class (the class of divine persons), but that they are members of one another, however extraordinary that may be. The three members of the Holy Trinity are akin to each other in these highly mysterious ways.

> *"The Trinitarian approach to God must always be important for Christian worship, as a safeguard against our worshiping an idol of our imaginations instead of the true God."*
>
> Donald Macpherson Baillie, *God Was in Christ* (New York: C. Scribner's Sons, 1948), p. 155

To believe in the oneness of God is not to believe that heaven is occupied by only one divine person.[8] Our Lord's analogy makes this clear. He prays for the church, that we may be one as he and the Father are one. And, of course, we are not one person. Our oneness is communal.

Perhaps we can describe this oneness more fully. First, all Christians can confess that our oneness in the church is a pale reflection of the kinship of Father, Son, and Spirit. For just as no divine person can be God without the other two, so no Christian can be the church without the rest of the body. A certain modern confession says, "Each member is the church in the world." But that's not quite right. None of us is the church without the rest of us. Instead, we are individually *members* of the universal church in the world — a church so vast, so deep, so old, so multinational, so wonderfully catholic that only the Lord of the universe can be its head.

---

8. Belief "in one person" is a classical form of the heresy of modalism.

Reasons for Being at Worship

Marva J. Dawn

Just as worship needs to be filled with details so that young people get a larger, more interesting view of God's splendor, so worship needs to be filled with reasons for them to be there. We have all heard the plaintive cry from kids, "Why do I *have to go* to church?" Here are some answers that I give them:

1. We're not *going to church;* YOU *are* the Church — and we go to worship so that we learn how to be Church.

2. We need you with us in worship because those who are old and tired need your smiles and vitality.

3. The congregation cannot get along without you. Just as your body needs every single part — like your eyes, your nose, your mouth, your hands and feet — so the Church needs every single person to make it whole. Perhaps this Sunday some persons will need you to be eyes or hands for them.

4. You need the gifts of worship because you will learn things there that will make sense later. Almost every week I learn something that comes up in the days that follow.

5. If you pay close attention to the words of the songs and the Scripture readings and the liturgy, you will learn all kinds of new things about God. Since God is infinitely incomprehensible, all of life is an adventure in getting to know him better, but worship is especially rich with his presence.

Second, what binds us together as one community is some semblance of the shared word, work, and will, the knowledge, love, and glory that fill the precincts of heaven. As we've seen, the oneness of God in the Fourth Gospel is communal. To speak of this oneness dynamically we will need the language of self-giving love (which "binds everything together," as Paul wrote). At the center of the universe, self-giving love is the dynamic currency of the Trinitarian life of God. The persons within God exalt each other, commune with each other, defer to one another. Each person, so to speak, makes room for the other two. It might sound a little strange, but we might almost say that the persons within God show each other divine *hospitality.* After all, John's Gospel says that the Father is "in" the Son and that the Son is "in" the Father (17:21), and that each loves and glorifies the other.

Early Christians in the Greek church called this interchange the mystery of *perichoresis,* and they added the Holy Spirit to the picture.

6. Attending worship will teach you skills for your Christian life — skills like how to pray, how to sing, how to sit quietly in God's presence, how to study the Bible.

7. I need you to come to worship because I have cancer and am taking chemotherapy, which makes me too sick to sing, so I need you to stand beside me and sing for the both of us. (This is not an answer I give right now, but it was a very important answer for three-fourths of a year.)

8. The congregation needs the talents you bring to worship — your singing voice in the hymns, your ability to learn new songs quickly, your ability to read the Scripture lessons well, your help with the ushering, your warmth and friendliness in the "Passing of the Peace," the answers you give during the children's sermon, your modeling of reverence for the other children. (This point makes us realize how much more all our churches need to do to engage the children more practically in the actions of worship.)

9. When I preach, I need to watch you to see if what I am saying is understandable to people your age. I need you to give me critiques when the worship service is over.

10. Most important, God needs you there because he loves to be with you in his house.

Excerpt from *A Royal "Waste" of Time: The Splendor of Worshiping God and Being Church for the World* (Grand Rapids: Eerdmans, 1999), pp. 256-57.

When they spoke of *perichoresis* in God, they meant to suggest that each divine person harbors the others at the center of his being. In a constant movement of overture and acceptance, each person envelops and encircles the others.

Supposing that hospitality means to make room for others, and then to help them flourish in the room you have made, perhaps we could say that hospitality thrives within the triune life of God and then spreads wonderfully to the creatures of God. The one who spreads it is a mediator, a person who "works in the middle." And to think of our union with Christ as also a union with God is to see that it is only through Christ, by the power of the Holy Spirit, that believers enter upon the Trinitarian life of God.

At the center of this life is self-giving love in triplicate interchange, a kind of hospitality that casts a whole new light on unity within diversity. In Christian eyes, this phenomenon means much more than simply giving everybody a place at the table. In the church, to seek unity is to enter the lives of people we love and invite them to enter ours, so that what once were special interests become mutual ones instead.

In *Taking the Word to Heart,* Robert C. Roberts offers an illuminating analysis of marriage that helps us understand self-giving love of this kind. What does it mean for two to become "one flesh"? Surely a Christian marriage is more than a contract between two people to stay together as long as each pulls value out of the other. Surely it's more than an agreement to serve each other's needs — emotional, sexual, companionable, and the rest. To become really one, a pair of human beings would have to make each other's interests their own — entering into them, trying to understand them, striving to appreciate them.[9] (He learns to play tennis so they can play together; she learns enough pottery to keep up with him.) Self-giving love is an adventure in which we enter the lives of others in order to give their joys, sorrows, and welfare a place in our heart.

> "We cannot be loved without being changed. When people experience love they begin to grow lovely."
>
> John Ortberg, *Love Beyond Reason* (Grand Rapids: Zondervan, 1998), p. 14

It sounds trite to say, given the recent history of the verb "share" within evangelical Christianity, but marriage is all about sharing the life of another. When a couple succeeds in this mission, the effect is powerful not only for themselves, and for their children, but also for countless others in the communities in which this couple dwells. Perhaps in an analogous way, the self-giving, unifying life of God, mediated to the church through Jesus Christ, may be wonderfully spread to those who attach to Christ by faith. To get "in Christ" is to gain a whole new way of life in which we no longer compete to prevail. Love does not "insist on its own way." Instead, the members of the body of Christ, full of the life mediated to them from God through Christ and his Spirit, strive to weep with those who weep, to rejoice with those who rejoice, and, in general, to cultivate those

9. Robert Campbell Roberts, *Taking the Word to Heart: Self and Other in an Age of Therapies* (Grand Rapids: Eerdmans, 1993), pp. 216-17.

community-building virtues that fit people who have died and risen with Christ in their baptism.

KOINONIA COMMUNITY

When the authors of the New Testament speak of such fellowship within the church, they refer to it as *koinonia*. This wonderful Greek term, with all its overtones of "having in common," of "sharing in common," appears prominently in Luke's account of Pentecost. When the Holy Spirit blew down the walls in people's hearts, they began to practice *koinonia* (Acts 2:42). They practiced fellowship. Jews from all over the Mediterranean basin began a common life as believers in Jesus Christ.

Some contemporary Christians have sometimes thought of sharing as little more than a password for talking about one's religious experiences ("I'd just like to share what the Lord has been doing in my life"), and of *koinonia* as roughly equivalent to singing "Kum ba yah" around a campfire. But in the New Testament, *koinonia* doesn't describe simple friendship among people who naturally get along together. Jesus called into fellowship disciples who wouldn't otherwise have had much to do with each other — even Matthew, whom Simon the Zealot must have once held in contempt. Matthew was, after all, a tax collector, a traitor whose vocation amounted to "giving aid and comfort to the enemy," not to mention to himself. The apostle Paul addressed his letters to churches riven by strife over ethnic identity and religious orientation: Shouldn't Gentiles be not only baptized but also circumcised? If we have liberty from the Law, does that mean we can do what we want? Are we disciples of Paul or Apollos?

On every occasion, Paul finds a way to say, Listen! Have you already forgotten *Christ*? Have you already forgotten that factions have no place in fellowship with him? Have you already forgotten that you should look not only to your own interests but also to the interests of others, since *this* is "the mind of Christ" (Phil. 2:1-5)? Have you forgotten?

Have we forgotten?

Faith in Jesus Christ includes faith in his program. The faithful person practices self-giving love, and trusts that he won't be a fool to do it. He practices humility, and trusts that humility is actually a sign of strength. She practices forbearance with people who drive her nuts, and trusts that forbearance is part of the image of God. Both come to a discussion quick to listen and slow to speak (James 1:19).

The point is that *koinonia* (and the virtues that make it possible) isn't an add-on to the gospel but an integral part of it. The good news is that Jesus Christ has reconciled the irreconcilable, has made peace where no one thought it possible. The good news is that between men and women, slave and free, Jew and Gentile, Jesus Christ has broken down the dividing wall of hostility (Gal. 3:28; Eph. 2:14).

The bad news is that his followers keep trying to put that wall back up. Some want women to preach; some do not. Some want the church to take a stand with unborn children; some want the church to stand with women in crisis pregnancies. Some think of old hymns as a gift; some think of them as a burden. In the worst cases, angry people get converted to Christ, as they gladly testify, and then simply import their anger into the church.

None of us should underestimate the difficulty of living our way into *koinonia*. Some things are worth fighting for, and some are not, but we still have to know which is which. Some differences among us are created by God and some caused by human sin, and, again, it's not always easy to sort them out.

But one fact remains. At Pentecost the Holy Spirit had to get through the armor of unrepentant hearts. In the church communities that Paul established, life in Christ seemed constantly at risk of unraveling as people's hearts hardened. To people who had died and risen with Christ in their baptism, Paul had to say, "keep doing it." Die to your anger, rage, malice. Die to factions, backbiting, quarreling. Rise to the new life of *koinonia* in Christ.

In this community, hostility gives way to hospitality. Instead of rebuilding the old dividing walls, we cut doors and windows into them, even when we aren't quite ready to let them come down. We want to overhear our brothers and sisters in the household, and we want to be overheard. We want to look not only to our own interests but also to the interests of others. In such a household, our identity is defined not by our surname, skin color, gender, age group, or even denomination. It is defined not by whether Twila Paris, Johann Sebastian Bach, or Kirk Franklin moves us or offends us. It is defined first by the fact that we are together children of God, and that we bear the indelible watermark of baptism, the seal of our adoption.

Even though our primary identity is as children of God, this doesn't mean that all God's children lose their individual identities. It doesn't mean that distinctions fade, that "the rainbow people of God," as Desmond Tutu calls us,[10] smear into a drab gray-green. Just the opposite. Where natural, God-given diversity is concerned, unity lets diversity come to life. A Christian community becomes a safe space for diversity. Embracing the healthiest feature of multiculturalism as a fact, a healthy church rejoices in natural diversity. We can't have the triune kind of life — including its kind of unity — without it. In this way godly unity presumes diversity. "Unity" does not apply to something of which there is just one, nor to identical things. The former is singularity, and the latter is uniformity; but neither singularity nor uniformity is unity.

St. Paul, who was obliged to think of this question from the start,

> *"Learning to live in unity with one another is a very organic thing. I believe firmly that worship is the place where we need to model unity, because worship, when it is truly worship, is at the same time the most naked and fully clothed moment in the life of a person and of a community. We are both vulnerable and secure when worship truly happens."*
>
> Jorge Lockward, in an interview with Emily R. Brink, "The More We Get Together," *Reformed Worship* 53 (September 1999): 23

10. Desmond Tutu, *The Rainbow People of God: The Making of a Peaceful Revolution,* ed. John Allen (New York: Doubleday, 1994).

produced an inspired image for the Christian community. The human body is made up not of one big part, nor of identical small parts, but of an assortment of parts that look nothing like each other at all. An eye here, a nose there; a kidney here, and a big toe there. Each part has its function, and none can do the others'. One sees, another smells. One is a waste treatment plant, and another steadies our posture when we walk. (Lose a big toe and the body begins to teeter.) In fact, it's some of the littlest parts that should get the greatest honor (1 Cor. 12).

"The scope of who it is that God means to invite to the feast, you see, is not ours to define. We are not put in charge of the guest list."

Don S. Skinner, from *Passage through Sacred History* (Cleveland: United Church Press, 1997), p. 93

But a body also needs a good head, one that will assure that all these motley parts will be able to work together. In the church, Christ's headship of the body is the necessary condition of the church's unity. As Calvin put it, "there could not be two or three churches unless *Christ* be torn asunder — which cannot happen!"[11]

So the church *is* one. Christ is the benefactor of this amazing gift, and we its beneficiaries. But, of course, here we have a little problem: Around 1054 A.D. the church split, East versus West, and then in the sixteenth century the Western church split again, not just once or twice, but again, and again, and then again. Ever since, denominations and nondenominations have proliferated into a bewildering array of "options," some of them the result of honest differences, but many the illegitimate children of the same old sins that should have died with Christ.

So where is Christian unity?

The response is sober and familiar. Christian oneness is as much a calling as it is a gift. It may be a fact, but it's also a goal. Our oneness, and the true *koinonia* that is its mark, are benefits of salvation that Paul calls us to work out with fear and trembling, not on our own strength, but on God's, and not for our own good pleasure,

---

11. Calvin, *Institutes*, 2:1014 (4.1.2).

A Cultural Ethic for Christian Worship

Melva Wilson Costen

The New Testament understanding of liturgy, which has suffered loss in translation, is that Christ's life, death, and resurrection are, in fact, the epitome of liturgy. Christians who claim that their lives are in Christ are formed and shaped by the likeness of Christ, and are an embodiment of efforts to make present this *one* liturgy in all times and places. This is to say that Jesus' life of worship as God incarnate, both in ritual actions and in ethical responses to the holy, is the ultimate model of worship. We truly worship as we are empowered by the Holy Spirit to embody Christ present in and through us.

The most effective demonstration of true liturgy is what we do in obedience to God in Christ with our lives when we gather and when we scatter as a community in the world. To participate obediently drives worshipers to earnestly desire both the assembly and the scattering. Life in the world always calls one back to mutual companionship in gatherings, confession of sin, pardon, and renewal. Empowered gathering evokes the need to go forth into the world to love and serve in spite of the fact that the world and the worshiper are unfortunately not always compassionate and loving.

As the Holy Spirit works through the people's work, transformation of time, worshipers, and the world are all made possible. No participation in ritual action, whether culturally understood or borrowed from other cultures, can be renewing if the intent of the Christ event is not rooted in a true desire of the worshiper to be transformed. If one approaches the holy meal with blinders so that those gathered at other tables are not also seen through the "mind's eye," regardless of differences, one cannot truly see Christ in one's neighbor.

Excerpt from *African American Christian Worship* (Nashville: Abingdon, 1993), pp. 127-28.

---

but for God's (Phil. 2:12-13). In good Christocentric form, Karl Barth once wrote that Christians who want unity must keep their eyes on the one who suffered and was raised to win it:

> The quest for the unity of the Church must in fact be identical with the quest for Jesus Christ as the concrete Head and Lord of the Church. The blessing of unity cannot be separated from Him who blesses, for in Him it has its source and reality, through His Word and Spirit it is revealed to us, and only in faith can it become a reality among us.[12]

12. Karl Barth, *The Church and the Churches* (Grand Rapids: Eerdmans, 1936), p. 28.

Space for Grace

Cindy K. Holtrop

Today we associate the word *stranger* with caution and fear. Don't talk to strangers, we tell our children. We look over our shoulder in parking lots. We watch our children carefully in stores and even in our own backyards. We do not easily welcome strangers into our homes or lives. We have good reason to exercise caution and discernment. But perhaps our wariness makes us miss opportunities for "entertaining angels."

Strangers, orphans, widows, and the poor were on God's priority list of people to receive hospitality in the Old Testament (Exod. 23:9; Deut. 10:18-19). These were the vulnerable people, the ones who were without the protection and care of their clan. By failing to practice hospitality toward these people, the Israelites aroused God's anger. The Israelites did not reflect the hospitable, gracious character of God that they themselves had experienced (Exod. 22:21-27). . . .

During Israel's years of wandering in the desert, during the years of disobedience, during the years of being shaped into a nation that God could use to reach the nations, God cared for and protected Israel. God commanded Israel to welcome strangers and to care for the poor, the widows, and the orphans out of gratitude for their deliverance. The most unlikely strangers — Rahab and Ruth, among others — became a part of Israel's faith family. God's welcoming vision for his kingdom always

Spelled out in ordinary language, faith in Jesus Christ and in his program allows us to express our God-given unity by letting each part of the body be itself, and by delighting in it and in its contribution to the whole. Remarkably, we may express our faith in the unity of the church by celebrating its legitimate forms of diversity. We don't just settle for what we've got going over here and let others settle into whatever seems to work for them over there. We don't set up our worship according to quotas, counting each other's psalms and hymns and spiritual songs with a jealous eye. Music is for praising God, not for dividing the church into clans. In healthy churches we die to our special interests and rise to the interests of brothers and sisters, whether they worship with us across the aisle, across the street, or across the country. We rise to their interests whether they worship somewhere else in the world, or even sometime else in history.

The family of God trots the globe and spans the centuries. In Christ, we are one with *whoever* trusts the promise of salvation in

extended beyond the borders of Israel.

In the New Testament, Paul refers to Gentiles and sinners as being alienated from God. But in Jesus Christ the dividing wall of hostility has been torn down. Once strangers to God, we are welcomed as friends through Jesus Christ (Rom. 5:6-11; Eph. 2:11-14; Col. 1:21-23). This is our motivation for welcoming people and for offering hospitality. Because we are members of God's family, we share God's passion for others to experience God's embrace of grace. Without this underlying motivation, we can easily become weary and discouraged.

Hospitality is an attitude that informs our practices and habits. It is made concrete in sacrificial acts of love where we lay down our lives for another person. How will we know when we are practicing hospitality? When it costs us something. The cost may be time – writing a note of encouragement, developing a relationship with a family member we have neglected – or perhaps it is sacrificing our pride and asking forgiveness, or even creating space on the road for the driver ahead of us.

When we practice hospitality (Rom. 12:13), we welcome Christ who welcomed us (Rom. 15:7). Our hospitality to strangers in Christ's name has eternal value, for someday Christ will welcome us with open arms into the eternal kingdom (Matt. 25: 34-40).

Sermon notes, excerpted from "Space for Grace: A Service with a Focus on Hospitality," *Reformed Worship* 59 (March 2001): 17.

Jesus Christ. Our union with Christ joins us not just with those who were baptized last Sunday morning, nor just with those to whom we passed the cup and the loaf. We are also one with Adam and Eve, and Abraham and Sarah, and David, Isaiah, and Ruth. We are one with Matthew, Mark, and Luke; and with the Parthians, Medes, and Elamites who were cut to the heart after hearing Peter's Pentecost midrash one windy day in Jerusalem. We are one with the martyrs, the reformers, and the revivalists. One with believers on every continent, yesterday, today, and tomorrow.

When we delight in our diversity by rising to the interests of others (and we'll see just what kinds of things our interests might rise to in a moment), we do so not for the sake of ideological conformity with the world, but for the sake of praising God, who welcomes the parade of nations into the holy city (Isa. 60; Rev. 21).

In the previous chapter, we took a little time to stop and smell the roses of both creation and then of the new creation. Perhaps we may think of our church worship as rehearsal for that great day. In worship we and others from around the world bring to God the personal and communal treasures of our hearts and lives — our faith, hope, and love.

In one of the most powerful speeches ever given in America, Martin Luther King Jr. interpreted for a divided nation the prophetic vision of shalom. From the steps of the Lincoln Memorial in Washington, D.C., in 1963, he declared, "I have a dream that one day the state of Alabama ... will be transformed into a situation where little black boys and black girls will be able to join hands with little white boys and white girls and walk together as sisters and brothers." King didn't dream of these little black and white children holding hands because holding hands would be a token expression of racial desegregation. King was thinking more prophetically. He dared to dream as he did because he knew that holding hands is simply what children do when they are free to play together. It's simply what they do when they haven't been conditioned to think of their skin color first, or to consider on which side of the tracks their family lives.

> *The grace of our Lord Jesus Christ, the love of God and*
> *the communion of the Holy Spirit be with you all.*
> *If you are spiritually weary and in search of rest;*
> *if you are mourning and you long for comfort;*
> *if you are struggling and you desire victory;*
> *if you recognize that you are a sinner*
> *and need a Savior —*
> *God welcomes you here in the name of Christ.*
> *To the stranger in need of fellowship,*
> *to those who hunger and thirst for righteousness,*
> *and to whoever will come —*
> *this congregation opens wide her doors*
> *and welcomes you in the name of the Lord Jesus Christ.*
>
> "A Greeting of God and Welcome for Worship," in Cindy K. Holtrop, "Space for Grace: A Service with a Focus on Hospitality," *Reformed Worship* 59 (March 2001): 16

For Christians, "holding hands," or investing in each other's interests, is what ought to come readily, just because we remember that we are *first* children of God and *then* whatever else we may be. We are children of God, who learn first to love what God loves, and then to seek those loves in the interests of our brothers and sisters.

Much is at stake. If we can't, or won't, live in *koinonia*, we lose not only peace but also peace of mind. The devil goes to church, and

Hospitable Leadership of Songs for Worship

John Ferguson

In today's culture congregational song is a remarkable, novel thing. Today the individual is supreme. In a culture of self-gratification and perpetual entertainment, the notion of singing together to each other in any corporate way is a radical one indeed. Reflecting on the apostle Paul's charge to the Romans — "Do not be conformed to this world, but be transformed by the renewing of your minds . . ." — we might say that congregational singing is a nonconforming, not-of-this-world, countercultural activity. It is a transforming act, and it is the duty and delight of the leader of congregational song to energize worshipers in it.

But what do we sing and how do we sing it? What are some of the basic issues that should be considered by a hospitable leader of congregational song?

Hospitality suggests a gracious concern for one's friends or guests. The hospitable song leader will care about singers by providing songs with good texts and good tunes. The hospitable song leader will understand the dynamics of group singing and will seek to lead in creative and enabling ways.

Of all these issues, the concern about text is primary. In our worship songs we communicate to God and tell each other about God. We tell of God's marvelous deeds and in the process praise God, the doer. It is vital that our texts be biblically, theologically sound. It is important that they have substance. There is nothing inherently wrong with a praise chorus: After all, such songs began at creation when the morning stars sang, continued at Christ's birth when the angels sang. They echo throughout all time as God's people have sung simple (but not simplistic) refrains of praise. Mary sang such a refrain when she learned she was to be the mother of God's own son: "My soul magnifies the Lord. . . ." But she went on to tell us *why* she was inspired to sing her chorus of praise. She sang

continued . . .

---

when the members let the devil divide them, one thing that happens is that everybody goes home depressed. What could be more depressing than fighting with other believers, and especially over the worship of God?

What's at stake? Peace of mind, but also, and more important, God's image. The image of God is social as well as personal, as we've learned from John 17, and the church has been called to reflect it. To do this is simply to act in character as the body of Christ. God, who is rich in mercy, has chosen to mediate self-giving love to human creatures through the work of Jesus Christ. It's therefore fitting for

of God's marvelous deeds of exalting the humble, of feeding the hungry, of turning the world's notions of success upside down.

It is easy and exciting to sing again and again words like "glorify" and "magnify." But Christians need to ask "Why?" and then to sing about the answer. It is important that Christians sing songs about the redemption story, songs that invite us to "ponder anew what the Almighty can do," as Joachim Neander once put it.

We also need sturdy tunes that carry texts well. We need tunes that are accessible, memorable, and singable. While the text is paramount, the tune is what makes the text come alive, what determines if the text lives or dies. Complex syncopations, difficult melodic leaps, and excessively wide melodic range make a tune difficult for a congregation to sing. These attributes have nothing to do with the genre of the music, but have everything to do with whether the congregation will sing them well and with confidence. Some tunes from choral anthems and some tunes from the Contemporary Christian Music scene are

equally inappropriate for just these reasons. Both may be intended more for performance and may be too complex to encourage the meaningful participation of an entire congregation. The point, then, is not the style but the nature of the harmony, melody, and rhythm. As Ralph Vaughan Williams once observed, there is a "moral rather than a musical issue" at stake with writing music suitable for congregational singing.

The hospitable leader of congregational song will also seek to understand the dynamics of such song in order to lead it well. Marvelous technique and the ability to perform well are not enough. The organist who plays Bach fugues magnificently or the praise band that can cover most any tune may not be the most hospitable song leader. This issue is not just musical competence, but knowing how to use musical skills in ways that enable and encourage, not disable and discourage, group singing.

Wrong notes, dropped rhythms, unclear introductions, lack of time to breathe at phrase endings — these things generate feelings of unease in a congregation. If they feel they cannot trust their

those who have been entrusted with this heavenly form of love to reflect it back to the one who gave it.

What's at stake? Peace of mind, the image of God, and, in the end, the church's very mission. The church is an agent of Christ, sent to do God's work in the world — preaching the gospel, making disciples, tending AIDS patients, lobbying for peace, caring for widows and orphans. All this requires united action. A church at war with itself, or divided into neat cells of parties agreeing to disagree, can't do its work very well.

The church's mission is also to help spread the new life by mod-

song leader, worshipers will withdraw from singing. The song leader must provide stable rhythm, time to breathe, and clear directions. Sometimes these directions are visual, but more often and significantly they are aural.

The absolute necessity for consistent and predictable song leadership must not be misconstrued as a demand for dull sameness. Just as everything in nature is in a state of constant, subtle flux, so the leadership of congregational song should be sensitive to the need for simple, subtle modifications, especially in hymns with multiple stanzas. Careful changes in instrumental color or harmonization can contribute to a more vital experience of communal song.

In this context, the hospitable song leader knows when to lead, when to follow, and when to get out of the way. Sometimes one must lead: presenting a new tune, or revitalizing an old one. Sometimes one must follow, or, better, accompany: singing's going well, so no need to be too powerful; just support and subtly encourage the congregation in its singing. Sometimes one must get out of the

way: some songs beg to be sung unaccompanied, either in harmony or in a stirring, strong unison.

A final facet that the hospitable leader of congregational song should control: the dynamic level. Sonic assault from an organ or a praise band will always lead to congregational silence. If overwhelmed by a full organ or by an overly amplified band, the congregation will withdraw. The unintentional message being sent is that the people aren't needed. And, of course, too radical a shift from loud to soft will confuse a congregation, too. If one wishes to lead a group into confident, unaccompanied singing, it is best to begin with them, and then "to run and hide," gradually fading away. By the time the absence of instrumental accompaniment is noticed, the congregation will be singing so confidently the lack of instrumental support will be irrelevant.

The creative and engaging leadership of congregational song is a marvelous opportunity to use all of one's musical skills and insights. It requires great sensitivity and has the potential to be enormously satisfying when "it all works."

---

eling it. My prayer, says Jesus in John 17, is not for these disciples alone.

> I pray also for those who will believe in me through their message, that all of them may be one. . . . May they also be in us so that the world may believe that you have sent me. . . . May they be brought to complete unity to let the world know that you sent me and have loved them even as you have loved me. (John 17:20-21, 23, NIV)

Church unity is a powerful model of the very life of God — *so that*

Cross-Cultural Actions in Worship

Melva Wilson Costen

If worshipers are deliberate in their attempt to incorporate ritual actions of others, they must be clear about *why* they want to do so. Ritual action cannot be injected (as with a hypodermic needle) into a community's liturgy or liturgical life. The corporate nature of the assembly is a decisive factor in the enhancement of liturgy. This must be clear as the starting point for an effective grounding of actions. Corporate worship is indeed an important starting place for worshipers to appropriate faith traditions so that the lived experiences of others

might be understood. African Americans have adapted and assimilated liturgical actions from other cultures by redefining the actions in the light of their own lived experiences. For some worshipers, the elimination of prejudices against certain cultures and people must begin with reeducation and reconciliation before learning can take place. A divinely empowered encounter with God at a deeper level, basic to worship, can take place as worshipers experience ritual action that evolved through another's faith experience.

Excerpt from *African American Christian Worship* (Nashville: Abingdon, 1993), p. 128.

---

the world may believe, to let the world know. Sad to say, church disunity arouses "the scornful wonder" of unbelievers who knew all along that churches are for hypocrites, and cranky ones at that.

KOINONIA AS A CHARACTERISTIC OF CHRISTIAN WORSHIP

In his book *Total Chess,* David Spanier notes that the number of unique, non-repeating forty-move chess games that can be played is much greater than the estimated number of electrons in the universe.[13] True for chess, it's also true for *koinonia.* That is, the number of distinct, nonrepeating opportunities we have in worship (as in the rest of life) to express our unity with believers throughout the world and throughout history is legion. Let's dream of just a few.

First, to fit in with Christ's program, *worship leaders speak hospitably.* God's Word became incarnate in order to redeem. Christ

13. David Spanier, *Total Chess* (New York: E. P. Dutton, 1974), p. 132.

is both the first word and the last, but in the meantime he has commissioned the church to speak good words of redemption and welcome. So worship leaders welcome all who have been redeemed, whether male or female, Portuguese, Sudanese, or Japanese. They welcome seekers who have not yet been redeemed, and seekers who have belonged to the church for thirty years. They speak not just of the "sons of God" and the "brothers in Christ" but of the "daughters" and the "sisters," too. Per-haps borrowing from good children's literature, they use language that's simple and deep at the same time, understandable to children and de-

> *"It is impossible for one to live without tears who considers things exactly as they are."*
>
> Gregory of Nyssa, *De Beatitudine* III.6

lightful to grandparents, and dignifying to both. In speaking of others' music and worship styles they speak respectfully, or at least inquiringly, but not dismissively. For example, they shun the tradi-tionalists' scorn of "praise ditties" and the contemporary scorn of "dead hymns."

Second, *worship leaders encourage a congregation's awareness that it is surrounded by the invisible cloud of witnesses that gathers with us in worship,* just because we are all one in Christ. This means welcoming the stranger and her ethnic treasures, such as songs, hymns, and spiritual songs. We learn to sing them the way she would sing them, maybe even clapping, swaying, and stomping to rhythms that seem out of sync with our own. This means using the hand-carved communion pieces missionaries brought to us from Zimbabwe, rather than leav-ing them as curios in a fellowship hall cabinet.

Being aware of the cloud of witnesses means praying for the needs of believers whose plight seems not to touch our own, always aware that when one part of the body suffers, the whole body suf-fers with it. So we pray for African-American churches of the South, threatened by arson; we pray for the Anglican Church of Canada, on the brink of bankruptcy. We North American Christians pray for Christians in southern Sudan, victims of a genocidal war with Muslims; we pray for believers in Iraq, who face an uncertain fu-

Glimpses of *Koinonia* Worship

• Worship planners in churches of every kind and style are motivated to attend not just the Hymn Society's conference, or Willow Creek's Arts Conference, or Hampton University's Ministers' and Musicians' Conference, but all three, in the same year, to reap a harvest of new ideas.

• Urban churches of differing ethnic backgrounds regularly participate in one another's services of worship.

• An ethnically homogeneous church in North America learns a setting of *Kyrie eleison* ("Lord, Have Mercy") composed in Ghana. Its minor mode and haunting sighs remind them of the plight of African Christians, while its Greek text, sung for two thousand years in both East and West, reminds them that the trust of all Christians is first in the mercy of the Lord. (This setting may be found in *Songs of the World Church,* ed. and arr. John Bell, vol. 1 [GIA Publications, 1992], p. 23.)

• A planner of a contemporary worship service chooses one ancient text – a hymn, a prayer, or a creed – to remind those who gather in the twenty-first century that they are one with those who gathered in the first.

• Projected headlines and images from the news are prompts for the prayers of the people.

• Whether they prepare the "contemporary service" or the "traditional service," worship planners in a single church gather weekly for prayer and for study about worship's meaning and purpose.

• A church, in an effort to reach its youth, heads down a path toward multiple services. During a congregational meeting, plans are tabled when one middle-aged member stands to say, "My children need to worship alongside my parents, and my parents need to worship alongside my children. Otherwise my family isn't complete, and neither is the family of God."

• During their educational hour, children are taught to sign a congregational response, such as, "The Lord be with you." "And also with you." The children in turn teach the congregation during worship.

ture. Across the world, many of these believers intercede for us in North America, praying that our faith might not be buried by our consumer goods.

In these ways worship can be interracial and inter-ethnic even in churches that can't help their local homogeneity. Given their time and place, such homogeneity seems to be their inheritance. But this doesn't prevent such churches from joining their hearts to the interests of believers across the world. Here's an opportunity to

- Artists of all ages are invited to offer pencil drawings, charcoal sketches, or original computer graphics for the covers of weekly worship folders or bulletins.

- A simple setting of "Jesus Loves Me, This I Know," played once through by a solo instrumentalist, concludes a baptismal prayer.

- The Lord's Prayer is offered, but each petition is interposed with a fitting prayer of believers of another age or on another continent or in another neighborhood:

> Leader: *Our Father in heaven, hallowed be your name, your kingdom come, your will be done, on earth as it is in heaven.*
>
> People: *O Lord our God, who has chased the slumber from our eyes, and once more assembled us to lift up our hands and to praise your just judgments, accept our prayers and supplications, and give us faith and love. Bless our coming in and our going out, our thoughts, words, and works, and let us begin this day with the praise of the sweetness of*

> *your mercy. Hallowed be your name. Your kingdom come. (Greek liturgy, third century)*
>
> Leader: *Give us today our daily bread.*
>
> People: *God, of your goodness give me yourself, for you are enough for me. And only in you do I have everything. (Julian of Norwich, fourteenth century)*
>
> Leader: *And forgive us. . . .*

- Members of the congregation, no matter what their age, are invited to read the Scripture text for the day. During the week before, they receive simple instruction from the minister or another worship leader about reading that particular text for the sermon that is being prepared.

- During a worship service in which the children will leave and disperse to their worship centers, they pause before departing to exchange a blessing with those who remain in the sanctuary: "The Lord be with you as you worship." "And also with you."

---

practice unity in diversity with awareness that in so doing we are like God.

Worship with some inter-ethnic, intergenerational, and international dimensions can take a number of forms, as the article "Glimpses of *Koinonia* Worship" above section illustrates. In some dim way, the Christian church may more and more express its unity, reflecting the unity of God, wherever believers have "the same mind" — that is, wherever they look not only to their own interests but also to the interests of others. The beauty of a big frame for understanding how to "do church" is that it opens us to the beauty of God, who loves not only all humankind but also all human kinds, and invites us to love what he loves.

Chapter 5

God's Story and Ours:
The *Worshiping* Church

BECAUSE OF ITS EXTRAORDINARY FORM of unity in diversity, the Christian church is an image of God, and is called to become a better one. The church's one foundation is Jesus Christ her Lord, her model is the holy Trinity, and her calling is to "live into" her multicultural oneness. Christ has called into fellowship an amazing assortment of believers — far and near, past and present, young and young at heart — whose church life is, in a way, like marriage. It's a school for learning to celebrate a shared life.

Some Latin American churches have developed a powerful means of expressing this *koinonia* in Christ. On Easter Sunday the names of martyred men and women are called aloud, and the whole congregation shouts in return, "*¡Presente!*" In that moment, the living and the dead are present, united in the benefits of Christ's death and resurrection, our only hope of salvation.

Juan Tamayo. *¡Presente!*

António Oliveira. *¡Presente!*

Maria Ibañez. *¡Presente!*

Aurélio Guevara. *¡Presente!*

Celebrating our union with saints and martyrs deepens Christians' sense of the church's density. But, thinking biblically, we could have the same Easter celebration by calling just one name. After all, Juan Tamayo, António Oliveira, Oscar Romero, Mother Teresa, Martin Luther King Jr., and our own faithful grandparents are all "in Christ." So at the name of Jesus the whole church shouts, "*¡Presente!*" We shout, not for ourselves alone, nor merely for our loved ones, but for every saint of every nation of every epoch for whom Christ died and with whom we therefore worship today.[1]

In Christ we share an indivisible communion with one another. But in Christ we also share an indivisible communion with the triune God. Christ was lifted up as a sacrifice for our sins, and now Christ by his Spirit lifts us up, with our sacrifice of praise (Heb. 13:15). This is a function of Christ's priestly role: to "lift us up into a life of communion, of participation in the very triune life of God," as Scottish theologian James B. Torrance once put it.[2] Here is the essence of Christian worship. As members of a people whose storyline includes creation, sin, and grace, we commune with our creator and savior — with God, through Christ, in the power of the Holy Spirit. *Worship is narrative engagement with the triune God.*

This last statement needs unpacking, and the process of doing so will give us the sections of this chapter. We'll begin with *worship:* what does it mean to worship, and why should we worship God? Next we'll think about *engagement:* in what ways do we "engage" with God when we worship? Finally, what does it mean that engagement with God is *narrative?*

---

1. This illustration is owed to Cynthia A. Jarvis's Easter sermon, "The Community of the Living and the Dead," preached April 23, 2000, at Chestnut Hill Presbyterian Church, Philadelphia, and located on the Internet at http://philanet.com/~ecarr/april23_sermon.html (May 2000). The illustration is originally from Jürgen Moltmann.

2. James B. Torrance, *Worship, Community and the Triune God of Grace* (Downers Grove, Ill.: InterVarsity, 1996), p. 32.

WORSHIP

Given that people use "worship" to refer to various phenomena, the term has become elusive in English. We often need context clues to know what we're talking about. One reference is common. Most churches, for instance, whether a hundred years old and located downtown on the corner of Fifth and Main, or three years old and meeting in a high school auditorium, will advertise their principal activities something like this:

SUNDAY WORSHIP
8:30 and 11:00

SUNDAY SCHOOL
9:45

Here, "worship" covers the whole series of events that happens during the hour or so that churchgoers gather on Sunday mornings (or Wednesday or Saturday evenings, as the case may be). What happens during this hour will vary from church to church, week to week, season to season, but in any case the sequence of song and message, prayer and sacrament will be called "worship."

But "worship" is more than just a noun in the English language. Robert Webber once emphasized this point with the title of a book: *Worship Is a Verb.*[3] Worship is something we do, and we do it during the hour referred to when we use "worship" as a noun. One part of a worship service is actual worshiping, the part in which we call attention to God's glory and humble ourselves before it.

In the last book of the Bible, the revelation to the apostle John gives us an extraordinary glimpse of such worshiping (Rev. 4). There we find John "in the spirit," seeing and hearing extraordinary things in the throne room of God. An emerald rainbow surrounds

3. Robert E. Webber, *Worship Is a Verb* (Waco, Tex.: Word, 1985).

the throne, and flashes of lightning and peals of thunder emanate from the throne itself. In front of the throne, seven torches flame and a crystal sea sparkles. Gathered around the throne, four living creatures — one each like a lion, an ox, and an eagle, and one with a human face — keep on proclaiming, "Holy, holy, holy! Holy, holy, holy!" Meanwhile, twenty-four elders leave their own thrones to fall before the one on the great throne. Having cast down their crowns in homage to the majesty of God, these elders *sing* (maybe in harmony so high and deep they make Jessye Norman sound like an alto and Russian basses like tenors):

> *You are worthy, our Lord and God,*
> > *to receive glory and honor and power,*
> *for you created all things,*
> > *and by your will they existed and were created.*

This is worshiping. This, in the parlance of Old English, is *weorth-scipe,* which means roughly "to ascribe worth to." What John sees is twenty-four elders "ascribing worth to God," not only in the words they speak but also in the gestures they embody. Everything they say and do says, *You, O living God, are worthy, and I am unworthy; you are great, and I am small; you are God, and I am not.*

These elders acclaim God's high status. They call attention to God's excellent character. They declare God's mighty acts. God is not only powerful, having "created all things," but also gracious, having willed all things into existence. God is the one who powerfully and generously enlarges the amount of *being* in the world. In the whole run of Scripture, God's power and grace are hard to tell apart. When the Psalms praise God's awesome deeds, we assume the psalmists have God's power in mind. After all, God rules the sun by day and the moon by night. God sets the stupendous bonfires that we call galaxies. God sets a bound to the restless sea. And sometimes the poets of God reflect on all this with awe:

When I look at your heavens, the work of your fingers,
    the moon and the stars that you have established,
what are human beings that you are mindful of them,
    mortals that you care for them? (Ps. 8:3-4)

The galaxies are the fingerwork of God, intricate as lace. But the mighty acts of God that believers celebrate are never just exhibits of sheer Godalmightiness. What bursts from Israel's songbook is glad awareness that God is good to the creatures of the earth — abundantly good, spectacularly good, unexpectedly good. The mighty acts of God are typically acts of mercy. It's so much like God to redeem life from the pit; so much like God to care for desolate animals; so much like God to move our transgressions way out to sea and bury them there.

> "A man can no more diminish God's glory by refusing to worship Him than a lunatic can put out the sun by scribbling the word 'darkness' on the walls of his cell."
>
> C. S. Lewis, *The Problem of Pain* (New York: Macmillan, 1962), p. 53

In the previous chapter we noted that the triune God is a mutually hospitable communion of three persons in their interlocking relations. In creation God marvelously extends hospitality to creatures. For such goodness, those around the throne ascribe to God "glory and honor and power."

We should not imagine that the elders invented such worthiness, as if it were not already part of God's character. No, to ascribe worth to God is, in a way, to bring coals to Newcastle, or diamonds to the Kimberly mines of South Africa. For what can human beings give to God that God does not already possess? The answer is nothing, if we're talking about glory, honor, power, or the very stuff of creation. Ascribing these things to God is reflecting them back to their Source, and word and song are merely the vocal ways of doing it.

This is one reason why many Christians employ another, broader use of the word "worship," in addition to the two we have already here explored. All of life is lived before the face of God, they say, so all of life is worship. In all that we do — whether preparing a sermon or a brunch, whether kneeling to pray or to find a child's toy beneath the bed — we may present ourselves "as living sacrifices," which is our "spiritual wor-ship," as Paul writes. We may "ascribe to the Lord the glory due his name," as the psalmist puts it, for whatever we do is our offering.

But if all life belongs to God, and if, in the splendor of the Holy Trinity, God has always been full of glory, what's the point of saying so? What's the point of ascribing back to God a worthiness God so obviously possessed before we even knew about it?

We might dutifully reply that God sovereignly requires our wor-ship, but that's at first glance a problem as much as an answer, and the problem arises in Scripture itself. In certain parts of the Old Testa-ment we find God on a soapbox, declaring his own accomplishments, blowing his own shofar. While the Israelites are trapped in Egypt, God repeatedly declares that "there is none like me in all the earth," and that Pharaoh will surely live long enough to know it: "I will get glory over Pharaoh!" Later, in Isaiah's prophecy, the Holy One lays out his resumé and then draws a seemingly immodest conclusion: "To whom then will you compare me, or who is my equal?" (Isa. 40:25).

Of course God *is* incomparable. No doubt. But shouldn't some-body else say so? Or shouldn't God, at least, manage his self-referencing a little more delicately? ("I know this will sound un-seemly, but the truth is I'm actually very great." Or, "you'll have to forgive a personal example, but there was a day when I. . . .") What we have instead is a God who calls attention to his greatness not to fish for compliments, but to demand them! In one way or another, God keeps saying to Israel: Forget about all those other gods, and worship me alone. After all, "who is my equal?"

Why does God talk like this? Why demand worship from hu-mans? What's the point? Surely it's hard to imagine that we are simply fulfilling a crude contract: We like goods, God likes worship — so tit-for-tat and call it good at that. Surely God cannot be like one of Philip Roth's narcissists, alternately fragile and grandiose — the kind of person whose ego needs to be pumped up whenever it loses pressure. After all, people made in God's image cannot conceivably be more mature than their maker.

But what if God requires worship not for God's sake, but for ours? Here's one way to look at it: Suppose a son strays from home and adopts a drug dealer as his parent-figure. The boy is with this dealer all the time, talking like him, walking like him, borrowing his Rolex, driving his Cadillac. The boy's mother watches with growing alarm. She has cleaned office buildings for years, just to satisfy her son's appetite and send him to a private school. She has made him do homework, take out the trash, and get enough sleep. She was determined to do all she could to insulate her son against the blandishments of easy money. She and her son have stood against the world. Now a stranger has gotten in between them.

> "Worship is God's gift to us, intended for our blessing and benefit. He doesn't need it; we do."
>
> Jack W. Hayford, *Worship His Majesty* (Ventura, Calif.: Regal, 2000), p. 250

Might there be a time when, given her history of care and self-sacrifice, this mother would have to lay out her resumé for her son? With quivering lip, this fine woman declares, "Son, don't neglect me. Don't forget that I'm your mother, and that there is no one else like me. There is no one like me on the street. I am the only one who really loves you and always will."

If we listened in on this mother's monologue, we wouldn't find her self-reference irritating. We would find it moving. She's out to save her son, and she'll do whatever it takes. We would be distressed that a situation could be so dire that this good woman would have to spread out her dossier for her son and remind him of what was obvious. And we would find in the reminder something more like humility than like pride.

In similar emergencies God's people hear God say, "Listen, don't neglect me. Don't forget that I'm your creator. Don't forget Egypt and the Exodus, and don't imagine that any of those other gods can save you." God knows that idolatry is not only staggeringly ungrateful but also heart-breakingly foolish. Idols can't carry you in the tough times. In fact, you have to carry *them*. And God lays out his resumé simply to help Israel answer the question, "Who is carrying whom?"[4]

4. We owe this expression to John Timmer.

God's Splendor

Marva J. Dawn

For a while this book *A Royal "Waste" of Time* was called *Immersed in Splendor.* I love the baptismal imagery in that phrase — like a plunge into a sapphire mountain lake on a hot day. Even so, worship is a cascade into the ever-flowing surprises of encounters with the immensity of God's magnificence and sublimity and radiance. We have retained the word *splendor* in the subtitle because worship that is a *royal* waste of time will immerse us in the fullness of God's sublime attributes and actions. That is why worship must be filled with all kinds of sounds, new music and old, faithful fountains of praise, powerful retellings of the biblical narrative, an ever widening river to convey the grandeur of God.

Surely one of the greatest problems of our times is that we have become so nonchalant about the Lord of the cosmos. Certainly if we were more immersed in God's splendor we should find ourselves thoroughly "lost in wonder, love, and praise" [from Charles Wesley's glorious hymn of 1747, "Love Divine, All Loves Excelling"]. With all the amazing sights and sounds of our cyberspace world, however, many of us no longer recognize that if we but catch a glimpse of *GOD* — the imperial Lord of the cosmos, the almighty King of the universe — we will be compelled to fall on our faces. Our awareness of God's absolute otherness would give us the sense that we could die now because we have seen God. We would shout with the prophet, "Woe is me, for I am annihilated" (Isaiah 6:5, Martin Luther's rendering).

The awe and astonishment of God's presence

As Jeremiah knew, human beings keep forgetting God. We turn our backs to God instead of our faces. God requires worship from us not to satisfy a divine inferiority complex but to help us remember who is carrying whom. Praise of God is an antidote to idolatry. Praise, as C. S. Lewis puts it, is "inner health made audible."[5] We might say that with respect to God, praise straightens our posture so that we neither strut nor slouch. No strutting — no forgetting that we need God's grace just to breathe or to do the smallest good deed. But no slouching either — no timid or depressed refusal to stand right up and approach the throne. Here's a paradox: to paraphrase Lewis, only weak people need God's goodness; only strong people are willing to say so. Exuberant worship of God indicates

5. C. S. Lewis, *Reflections on the Psalms* (New York: Harcourt, Brace and World, 1958), p. 94.

so far beyond us is so immense that we could hardly react with anything less than fear and trembling and the sacrifice of all our lives. Our superhyped culture makes it difficult for us to take the immense sovereignty and preeminence of *GOD* seriously; we find it hard to realize that his infinite splendor would overwhelm us if he weren't so gracious as to give us samples of it in small morsels. As with Moses, we really see only God's "back" or the *glory* of where he has been and how he has worked (Exodus 33:17-23).

Such taking God seriously is, however, decidedly countercultural. We live in an age and a culture that want instead to turn the worship of God into a matter of personal taste and time, convenience and comfort. Consequently, we need the biggest dose of God we can get when we gather for worship on Sunday morning — to shake us out

of this societal sloth and somnambulism and summon us to behold God's splendor and respond with adoration and service and sacrifice.

Taking God seriously, being immersed in his splendor, unites us with a community that practices the alternative way of life of following Jesus, of participation in the kingdom of God. That is why I use the phrase *being Church*. When we come to belief or are baptized (my concern here is not to deal with denominational or doctrinal differences), the eternal reign of God begins in our life. Thus also begin both the transformation of our character and the responsibility for the whole community to nurture our eschatological life.

Excerpt from *A Royal "Waste" of Time: The Splendor of Worshiping God and Being Church for the World* (Grand Rapids: Eerdmans, 1999), pp. 7-8.

that we know both *who* we are and *whose* we are. Once we know, we want to worship.

So worship, in the narrow sense of "ascribing worth" to God, is an essential part of worship in the broad sense of "what churchgoers do when they gather in the sanctuary on Sundays." But this narrow sense of the word "worship" isn't *all* that happens in the sanctuary on Sunday mornings, or Saturday nights, or Wednesday evenings. Nor should it be.

WORSHIP IS ENGAGEMENT

When God's people gather to sing, pray, hear the Word, and offer gifts, they expect to meet God. They anticipate an encounter with the living God, who descends to us, reminds us why we need him, and summons our fellowship.

God calls, and Love bids us welcome, as George Herbert put it. This is holy grace, and it warrants awe. This is God, who is worthy of exuberant praise tempered with reverence. What's called for is exuberant reverence, or reverent exuberance — some mix of boundless enthusiasm for God's grace and humble awareness of how much we need it. Attachment to Jesus Christ gets us deep into God, very close to God. But because it is God we approach, believers reject anything that looks like flippancy. Chatty prayers, jokes about God, and references to "the Big Guy" demean both the giver and the receiver. The incarnation licenses boldness, not sauciness. As we saw in the third chapter, the incarnation is a sign of God's strength, both in grace and in judgment, and it invites from us beneficiaries both love and reverence.

The triune God is both the one whom we worship and the one who enables our worship. It's not as if we convene ourselves and then wait for God to show up because we have said the magic words or cranked up enough volume in our praise. It's not *we* who summon God in worship, but *God* who summons us.

> "On the whole, I do not find Christians, outside of the catacombs, sufficiently sensible of conditions. Does anyone have the foggiest idea what sort of power we so blithely invoke? Or, as I suspect, does no one believe a word of it? The churches are children playing on the floor with their chemistry sets, mixing up a batch of TNT to kill a Sunday morning. It is madness to wear ladies' straw hats and velvet hats to church; we should all be wearing crash helmets. Ushers should issue life preservers and signal flares; they should lash us to our pews. For the sleeping god may wake someday and take offence; or the waking god may draw us out to where we can never return."
>
> Annie Dillard, *Teaching a Stone to Talk* (HarperPerennial, 1982), pp. 58-59

God calls, and in Christ by the power of the Holy Spirit we are drawn into divine fellowship, holy engagement with the holy God.

We have employed the word "engagement" several times now, and readers will have a natural sense of its meaning. It's a good word to use for worship. For one thing, "engagement" (and its root) suggests a coming together of two or more disparate parties. It suggests a rendezvous, which is what worship is: a rendezvous between God and God's people. As we'll soon see, this is a rendezvous in which all parties participate mutually and actively. That's the other virtue of using the word "engagement" for worship: it (especially its root) suggests activity and involvement. A woman is "engaged in espionage." A man has four "speaking engagements" in two weeks. A man and a woman get "engaged to marry," and they may find themselves pretty busy. *Worship Is a Verb,* said Robert Webber, and "engagement" helps us keep this in mind.

So what exactly are we doing in worship? What's the nature of our engagement?

Though Scripture doesn't answer such a question directly, it does offer clues, and many who have explored them have suggested that worship is a holy dialogue. Conversation partners include the triune God and the company of believers, the communion of the saints. When the church gathers for worship, "I" becomes "we," and personal experience gives way to a communal fellowship of those physically or spiritually present.

The fellowship dimension is crucial, and follows from the fact that it's impossible for someone to be in union with Christ by himself. Christ by the Spirit mediates both our fellowship and our worship, and keeps our worship from narrowing down to a personal practice. Seen merely as a personal practice, worship becomes what *I* do before God. *I* praise, and *I* pray. The sacraments, or ordinances, are memorials of *my* experience, *my* conversion, *my* faith, based on *my* attempt to attain to God. If a personal encounter and its psychic benefit are premier reasons for participating in worship, then the church becomes less and less a community of faith in Christ, and more and more a gathering of individuals who think a joint experience of worship gets them a better personal buzz. But "more important than our experience of Christ is the Christ of our experience," says James B. Torrance,[6] and he's right. Good feelings are a

---

6. Torrance, *Worship, Community and the Triune God,* p. 34.

Real Presence

John Wilson

In Deuteronomy 12, the Lord instructs his people to break down the altars where "the nations" serve their gods. Instead, they are to worship at the places God will designate.

> You shall go there, bringing there your burnt offerings and your sacrifices, your tithes and your donations, your votive gifts, your freewill offerings, and the firstlings of your herds and flocks. And you shall eat there in the presence of the Lord your God, you and your households together, rejoicing in all the undertakings in which the Lord your God has blessed you.

Here is the essence of worship. God is always present, but in worship he calls us to a heightened collective awareness and acknowledgment of his presence. And for Christians, the essence of the essence is the Eucharist. In his book *Holy People* (Fortress Press, 1999), Gordon Lathrop reflects on Irenaeus' liturgical theology. For Irenaeus, writes Lathrop, "the very bread and cup of the thanksgiving meal, which are the body and blood of the Lord and which nourish our own flesh and blood, proclaim the truth of the God who created the world and redeemed it in Jesus Christ."

So in the Eucharist we see Christian worship in its most concentrated form—"not just the Lord's Supper," Lathrop writes, "isolated and considered as one illustration of the Christian message. Rather, Eucharist is the whole economy of word set next to meal, texts set next to preaching, thanksgiving set next to eating and drinking, which makes up the deepest ecumenical pattern for celebration."

Perhaps what is most striking in the current debate over worship, then, is what hasn't been said. The Lord's Supper, Eucharist, the essence of the essence of God's presence, is so little mentioned. As Edward Farley observes in his article "A Missing Presence" (*Christian Century,* 18-25 March 1998):

---

fine by-product of focusing upon Christ in worship, but they are not the goal. To focus our devotion on Christ is to "present ourselves as a living sacrifice" both to Christ and to the body of Christ. People who present themselves in these ways sometimes feel good about it, and sometimes not, but in either case they have actually worshiped.

As one body, in union with Christ and in the fellowship of the Holy Spirit, we come before God in expectation of dialogue, an actual give-and-take exchange between God and God's people. Biblical worship flows like a purposeful conversation, during which we speak, but only because we have been spoken to. In a classic form of the dia-

To attend the typical Protestant Sunday morning worship service is to experience something odd, something like a charade. The discourse (invocation, praises, hymns, confessions, sacred texts) indicates that the event celebrates a sacred presence. But this discourse is neutralized by the prevailing mood, which is casual, comfortable, chatty, busy, humorous, pleasant, and at times even cute. This mood is a sign not of a sacred reality but of various congregational self-preoccupations.

I don't entirely agree with Farley's critique. Like many who sense that something is awry in our worship, he is too quick to diagnose "congregational self-preoccupations." But I believe that Farley's essay, with its haunting title, points us in the right direction.

∽

The sanctuary . . . was dark and unbeautiful, corresponding to a certain early 20th c. conception of churchiness. But the service on this weekday night . . . was different in some ways from that remembered past . . . .

True, there was a bulletin. There I could read, under the heading "Prelude," that the music we were hearing was, first, "Jesus Walking on the Water" (Violent Femmes, 1983), and, second, "Mercy Is the Mansion" (House of Mercy Band, 1999).

House of Mercy is a house of the spirit (and the Spirit), based in Saint Paul, Minnesota, but not of fixed abode. This House will set up shop in a Lutheran church or a coffeehouse, wherever there is an invitation. "House of Mercy started as an experiment," an insert in the bulletin explained, "like a show you put on in your parents' basement, or a club that meets in your garage. Our questions: Can we grow a church not by a formula devised by an 'expert' but by

logue, God issues an invitation, a call to worship: "Worship the Lord with gladness; come into his presence with singing"; and we respond, "For the Lord is good; his steadfast love endures forever. . . ." God longs for reconciliation with and among his children, and so we confess our sins and lament their effects. God assures us we have been forgiven in Christ, and we renew our commitment to live faithfully. Before Scripture is read, we call upon the Spirit to illumine our minds and soften our hearts. God speaks, through the ancient text that is opened and the message that is preached. Thanks be to God, we may hear in the message the Word of the Lord. God seals his promises in the cup of

recovering vital resources the contemporary
church seems to have lost, namely the recov-
ery of theology, the renewal of liturgy, and
active participation in the world?"

We sang, in the course of the service,
a gospel song, a spiritual, and the old Irish
hymn, "Be Thou My Vision." The sermon
was a team affair, out of Saturday Night
Live by Saint Augustine. There was incense
from a thurible. And at the center of worship,
there was Communion.

In recent years I've been to a number of "alternative" services that resemble this, not in most of
their particulars but in the hunger that drives them.
Yes, the rhetoric can be off-putting in its sweeping
condemnation of the dreaded status quo, but the
hunger is genuine, the thirst, I believe, for God's
presence. Is it surprising, then, that such alternative
liturgies often include the Eucharist?

In *Christianizing Death* (Cornell University
Press, 1990), Frederick Paxton tells us that "the
central act of preparation for death in the Roman
church of antiquity was the reception of the Eucharist under one or both forms as a 'viaticum'—that is,
a provision for the journey to the other world."

The churches that raised me—mostly Baptist,
with a deep conviction of the authority of Scripture—
would have decried this early Christian practice as
a superstitious accretion, a kind of syncretism. The
Roman church! How soon the rot set in! And so on.

Now that dismissal of "superstition" seems
quite wrong, and wrong in a way that's instructive.
Let us return to the "typical Protestant Sunday
morning worship service" as rendered by Edward
Farley. Yes, there *is* "something odd" there. Aren't
we determined to keep mystery at bay, even
though our "discourse (invocation, praises, hymns,
confessions, sacred texts)" says otherwise?

The Eucharist is likely to challenge us precisely
in its flagrantly supernatural claims. "Jesus said to
them, 'Very truly, I tell you, unless you eat the flesh

salvation and the waters of baptism, tangible gifts by which we taste
and see that the Lord is good. We pray — for ourselves, the church,
and the world — and we offer our gifts. Having had the first word,
God also has the last: a blessing of grace and peace.

Thinking of worship as dialogue is basic, and we'll continue to think
about it this way in the discussion that follows. But we shouldn't imagine that each item in a service of worship may be neatly assigned to one
party or the other. The dialogue is more complicated than this. Because
worship is communal, sometimes the community addresses itself. We
speak to one another in worship, spurring one another on in love and
good deeds, encouraging one another, just as the author of Hebrews

of the Son of Man and drink his blood, you have no life in you. Those who eat my flesh and drink my blood have eternal life, and I will raise them up on the last day; for my flesh is true food and my blood is true drink'" (John 6:53-55). John says that when they heard this, many of the people who had been following Jesus dropped out. "This teaching is difficult. Who can accept it?" It proved too difficult for the makers of the *NIV Study Bible*, whose notes explain that this passage has nothing to do with the Eucharist—and where did you get that idea, anyway?

What would a recovery of the Eucharist look like? For many churches—such as the one where my wife and I are members, Faith Evangelical Covenant Church in Wheaton—there is first the simple matter of frequency. Frequent communion (not once a month) is a necessary but not sufficient condition. Then the full meaning of the Eucharist—not of just the Lord's Supper—must be conveyed, again and again and through many channels, to the entire congregation.

Recovery of the Eucharist also entails a renewed commitment to telling the full story of God's revelation, from creation to new creation. Worship must reflect the whole arc of Scripture, so that we feel in our very bones the connection between those words in Deuteronomy, for example—"And you shall eat there in the presence of the Lord your God, you and your households together, rejoicing in all the undertakings in which the Lord your God has blessed you"—and what we are doing today when we take the bread and the wine.

"In the presence of the Lord your God." That is the astonishing claim at the heart of worship, and it provides a way to think about worship that sidesteps the traditional/contemporary polarity. How is worship in this place or that, in these particular local circumstances, consistent (or not) with the fundamental conviction that God, the mighty God, is present among us, his people?

---

commends (Heb. 10:24-25). *People* lead our worship. Ministers and worship leaders sometimes speak for God to us and sometimes speak to us for God. Sometimes the people do the same for one another.

So worship brings together a cast of more than two. It also arouses more than just a few human "affections," as Jonathan Edwards called them. Worship arouses a complex of our emotions, appraisals, enthusiasms, reflections. As Nicholas Wolterstorff has observed, praise is only one way to engage God because it reflects only one part of our life's experience. In an essay entitled "Trumpets, Ashes, and Tears," Wolterstorff notes that while we leave our homes, offices, and playgrounds to assemble in the sanctuary, "we do not leave behind our *experience*" of life in these arenas. "A fundamental dimension of the liturgy," he says, "is that in it we give expression, in concentrated and condensed ritualized form, precisely to our experience in the world and our response to that experience."[7] As the title of his piece suggests, Wolterstorff explores three ways that this is so, three dimensions of worship that engage us not only with God but also with our own lived experience.

The first dimension is one that we have already explored, namely, praise. To be human, says Wolterstorff (with an appreciative nod to Calvin) is to be "one of those points in the cosmos where God's goodness finds its response in gratitude."[8] Gratitude is the *fitting* response to goodness — so much so that an ungrateful person is as much a puzzle as an annoyance.

In one of his sermons, Douglas Nelson, for two decades minister of New Haven's First Presbyterian Church, tells of a Salvation Army band playing out in the rain on a street corner.[9] The uniformed band was soaked and a little bedraggled. Still, they did manage to toot and honk their way through a couple of hymns. But "one man didn't toot. He blared." He blasted away on his trombone, ruining the balance and harmony of the ensemble. This player was "a hulking tough, with a red, bloated face and a prizefighter's nose. Someone spoke to him afterward about his zest, and the man beamed." Then he lifted his trombone and said, "Listen, mister, when I think what God has done for me, I could blow this thing out straight!"

"Love the Lord your God with all your heart, and with all your

> "[T]hat the Word may not beat your ears in vain, and that the sacraments may not strike your eyes in vain, the Spirit shows us that in them it is God speaking to us, softening the stubbornness of our heart, and composing it to that obedience which it owes to the Word of the Lord. Finally, the Spirit transmits those outward words and sacraments from our ears to our soul."
>
> John Calvin, *Institutes of the Christian Religion* 4.14.10

---

7. Nicholas Wolterstorff, "Trumpets, Ashes, and Tears," *Reformed Journal* 36, no. 2 (February 1986): 19.

8. Wolterstorff, "Trumpets, Ashes, and Tears," p. 19.

9. From an unpublished sermon preached in the late 1960s.

soul, and with all your strength, and with all your mind," said Jesus (Luke 10:27), and what better way to do it than to try to blow the kinks out of your horn! Praise in worship is the soul's natural enthusiasm for God.

Still, no matter how hard we blow, there is one noise that is tough to drown out. The dissonance of evil persists right through the harmony of praise, and is not easily resolved. Nobody who goes to church leaves the memory of evil outside the door. Members of one racial group kill the spirits, and sometimes the lives, of another. Third World nations languish beneath debt service to first-world economies. An oil spill off the Alaskan shoreline, smog in major metropolitan areas, indiscriminate clear-cutting of rain-forests — all creation, says the apostle Paul, awaits the day when it "will be set free from its bondage to decay and will obtain the freedom of the glory of the children of God" (Rom. 8:20-21).

> "[T]he sermon is a vehicle through which God speaks in worship in a distinctive way. . . . the eternal Word of God connects to the present moment of worship through the proclaimer's words. . . ."
>
> Gary A. Furr and Milburn Price, *The Dialogue of Worship: Creating Space for Revelation and Response* (Macon, Ga.: Smyth and Helwys, 1998), p. 12

While even nonbelievers are impressed by moral evil in our world, believers experience something more. Believers, as Wolterstorff observes, experience the moral evil of humanity as waywardness, as alienation from God. They experience it as sin.[10] So while believers might join nonbelievers in boycotts and teach-ins, they also respond to moral evil with sorrow that they have grieved God, and therefore with a plea to God for mercy and deliverance. Along with trombones, believers come to worship "bearing the ashes of repentance."[11] We confess our guilt, for what we have done and for what we have left undone. We confess our sins, and the sins of our world, and we plead *Kyrie eleison* — Lord, have mercy — perhaps to the tune of a Ghanaian plainsong.

Praise and penitence belong together in biblical worship. But

10. Wolterstorff, "Trumpets, Ashes, and Tears," pp. 20-21.
11. Wolterstorff, "Trumpets, Ashes, and Tears," p. 21.

How Will We Respond?

Michael S. Hamilton

There is nothing we can do to do stop the new worship divisions, any more than we could stop the doctrinal divisions over who, when, and how to baptize. So the question is: How will we respond to the new tribalism of worship and music? How can we keep our sectarian worship from becoming a sectarianism of the soul?

First, we need to remember that differing expressions of Christianity are not necessarily a bad thing. For decades, theologians have wrung their hands over America's ecclesiastical fragmentation. "Denominationalism . . . represents the moral failure of Christianity," claimed H. Richard Niebuhr in *The Social Sources of Denominational-*

ism. Well, maybe. In fact, the United States, with the most denominationally divided Christianity of the Western world, also has the highest levels of Christian faith in the Western world. This empirical reality has led some people recently to wonder if the organizational splintering of the American church has not, in fact, been a strength as well as a weakness. The advantage of multiple expressions of Christianity — whether they are based in doctrine or based in worship — is that there is an expression for everyone. Anyone can find a home. And in this world of brokenness and homelessness, maybe having many different homes is a good thing.

Second, it is right and good to put different expressions of orthodox Christianity to a functional test rather than a theological test. Every complaint about worship music, no matter which style, claims

---

there's another emotion that belongs in worship, suggests Wolterstorff: genuine grief. After all, not every suffering can be explained as the simple fallout of our own sin and therefore responded to with personal confession. Consider a child who dies of SIDS. Or a woman assaulted with racial slurs. She suffers as the consequence of a moral evil, but not her own.

In the face of this sort of evil, says Wolterstorff, we grieve. We *lament.* We storm the gates of heaven, demanding a hearing in God's hall of justice. Taking our cues from the poets and prophets of the Old Testament, we may praise God on the same occasion that we lament evil, but we don't dismiss our pain. Pain and grief and suffering are the real experiences of life, and so we ought to give them a real voice in worship. "For worship to be truly contextual," writes Pedrito U. Maynard-Reid, "it must address those social sins that God truly hates, and let 'justice roll down

to be rooted in theological principles. Yet in every critique, the theology aligns perfectly with the critic's own musical taste. What may be more helpful instead is a pragmatic test based on a bit of wisdom from the Gospels: "The tree is known by its fruit." If this is so, then worship music ought to be judged not by the songs themselves but by the people who sing them. Looking at the songs themselves is rather like looking at the bark of a tree and then pronouncing the tree good or bad. Better to look at the fruit itself — the lives of the people who are singing the songs. The job of the local church is to communicate the good news of Jesus Christ, to draw people into a living relationship with God, and to remold disciples of Jesus into a Sermon-on-the-Mount shape. Any worship music that aids a church in these tasks is almost certainly a conduit

of the Holy Spirit. In light of this, maybe it is time to substitute charity for condescension.

Another path out of the wilderness of disdain is to begin to see others' music with new eyes. When the hymn reformers introduced music from other cultures into their canon, a handful of them noticed that the characteristics of praise and worship music that they most disliked are abundantly present in Christian folk songs from Africa, Latin America, and Asia. Many of these international songs have simple music, driving beat, repetitive lyrics, light theology, and an emphasis on experience. Here is a South African folk song that appears in the current United Methodist hymnal:

continued . . .

---

like waters, and righteousness like an ever-flowing stream' (Amos 5:24)."[12] Unfortunately, that's not typically what happens in our worship:

> Though we bring our tears of pain with us to our worship, we don't know how to cry them there. Tears in the assembly are regarded as liturgical failure. I suggest instead that a liturgy without tears is a failure. We must find a place for lament.[13]

Why? Because God is a suffering God, and the disciple is not greater than the master. If God suffers, so will those who have been created

---

12. Pedrito U. Maynard-Reid, *Diverse Worship: African-American, Caribbean, and Hispanic Perspectives* (Downers Grove, Ill.: InterVarsity, 2000), p. 49.

13. Wolterstorff, "Trumpets, Ashes, and Tears," p. 22.

Send me, Jesus, send me, Jesus, send me, Jesus,
   send me, Lord.
Lead me, Jesus, lead me, Jesus, lead me, Jesus,
   lead me, Lord.
Fill me, Jesus, fill me, Jesus, fill me, Jesus,
   fill me, Lord.

An openness to simple, repetitive international songs like this opened some reformers to accepting contemporary praise music produced domestically.

Meanwhile, a parallel movement is taking place on the other side of today's church music divide. Several musicians working out of the praise and worship genre are beginning to explore and appreciate music from different cultures around the world — including the classic English hymnody. The revolutionaries are already starting to include such hymns in their catalogs. One hopes it will not be long before they begin to draw upon the best of contemporary hymnody as well.

Does an openness to the varied musical expressions of different Christian cultures and subcultures leave us stuck in relativism, the tar baby of contemporary secular thought? By no means. It is merely to remember that the God who created this world did so with exuberant extravagance, his unchanging purpose often hidden in a tumbling cascade of variety. The resulting multiplicity has, ever since, been the medium of an infinitely dexterous Holy Artist, furthering the work of redemption in whatever cultural form human beings have been able to devise.

The Bible has four different Gospels; no single one of them tells us the whole truth about the life of Jesus. Likewise, no single musical style brings to full

in God's image. If Jesus Christ had to die before he was raised, so do those who follow Jesus.

Because authentic life provokes a range of acts and responses, so will authentic worship. It may include praise, penitence, lament; adoration, confession, intercession; and all the emotions that fit them.

All the gestures, too. Gestures give weight to our words. Sometimes they speak without words. Depending on the context, open palms may say, "I don't have a clue" or "Fill me, Lord" or both. Gestures affect our own sense of what we are saying. Imagine saying, "*I am a human being!*" first standing, your face turned to the skies and your fist shaking in the air; then fallen forward, on your hands and knees, your head bowed to the ground. You'll notice a difference.

So it is in worship and prayer. We may express praise not just with our voices, whether singing or speaking, but also with our arms upraised. We may express penitence not merely with hushed tones, but

flower more than a few of the many possibilities for communion with God. It is said that when King George II of England heard Handel's Hallelujah Chorus for the first time, it was not the glory of the music that – to the astonishment of the audience – pulled him to his feet. It was, rather, the glory of the Lord, surging through the conduit of the music. It was much the same when my elderly neighbor Elsie Hudson lay for several days in a coma. She responded to no one, not even her closest family members, until her pastor sat beside her and softly sang the simple gospel songs that she had sung all her life. The power of God surged through that music also – to the astonishment of the hospice workers – waking her up one last time before she went home to her Lord.

It is fruitless to search for a single musical style, or even any blend of musical styles, that can assist all Christians with true worship. The followers of Jesus are a far too diverse group of people – which is exactly as it should be. We need, rather, to welcome any worship music that helps churches produce disciples of Jesus Christ. We need to welcome the experimental creativity that is always searching out new ways of singing the gospel, and banish the fear that grips us when familiar music passes away. For this kind of change is the mark of a living church – the church of a living God, who restlessly ranges back and forth across the face of the earth seeking out any who would respond to his voice.

Excerpt from "The Triumph of Praise Songs," *Christianity Today* 43, no. 8 (12 July 1999): 34-35.

---

also with bent knees and bowed heads. Blessings may be signed, and songs choreographed in dance. "The body ought to pray as well as the soul," as C. S. Lewis writes in his *Letters to Malcolm.* In fact, "body and soul are both the better for it."[14]

But, of course, while gestures may enhance our worship, they may also distract us from it. Thus, once more, we need discernment to determine what actions fit our worship. In his Sermon on the Mount, Jesus warns his followers not to be taken in by lavish displays. People who trumpet their gifts ("Listen, mister, when I think what I have done for the Lord, I could blow this thing . . .") don't necessarily impress God. People who shout on street corners don't get God's attention before people who whisper at their bedside. People who thin themselves down by fasting, and then admire

14. C. S. Lewis, *Letters to Malcolm: Chiefly on Prayer* (New York: Harcourt, Brace and Company, 1992), p. 17.

their thin, new look, do not make the children of God shout for joy. Almsgiving, praying, and fasting are essential disciplines, but they are easily detachable from true worship of God.

In the same way, raising hands in praise, kneeling in prayer, and dancing for joy let the body worship as well as the mind, but these things may be done by a person whose mind is entirely somewhere else. Sometimes the body goes off on its own. Worse, gestures become expectable in certain worship settings to such a degree that they reflect spiritual tyranny and invite hypocrisy. "If I don't raise my hands, they'll think I've quenched the Spirit." "If I don't kneel, they'll think I'm too proud to repent."

How liberating it would be if Episcopalians praying from the Book of Common Prayer would feel free to raise their hands in exuberance at God's mighty acts without worrying that "this is not done" among Episcopalians. How liberating if worshipers in the Assemblies of God felt free to kneel in silence during the reading of a great old confession of sin, without worrying that "this is not done" in the Assemblies. How liberating if people's bodies naturally followed their spirits, and naturally followed scriptural affections and practices. Maybe this would be a new form of the unity Jesus prayed for in John 17. Maybe this would be a ground-level example of shared life — prompting a whole new ecumenical movement. Episcopalians and Assemblies together. Or what if Roman Catholics, like many of their Reformed brothers and sisters, remained in their seats during the Eucharist, passing the body and blood of our Lord to one another saying, "The body of Christ for you" and "The blood of Christ for you"? Or what if Reformed folk processed to the front of their church to partake of the elements, and there received these words of grace from the lips of their minister?

To worship with the whole person, body and soul, is to follow God's calling. Paul says that God appointed some to be apostles, and

> "To worship is to change. If worship does not propel us into greater obedience, it has not been worship."
>
> Richard J. Foster, *Celebration of Discipline* (San Francisco: Harper and Row, 1978), p. 148

Sung Prayer

C. Michael Hawn

Surprising as it may seem, singing is mentioned infrequently in the New Testament and in the documents of the early Christian church. This may be in part because in the culture and language of ancient Israel there was not a word for music in the more specific contemporary sense.

There is another perspective worthy of consideration, however. Singing may have been referenced rarely because it was assumed that when one prayed, one also sang. Edward Foley suggests in his book *Foundations of Christian Music* (Pastoral Press, 1992) that "there was . . . no sharp distinction between the sung and the spoken, no clear division between what we might call the musical and the non-musical, nor any denial of the fundamental lyricism of Christian worship"

(p. 84). Liturgical scholar Paul Bradshaw, who has examined most of the existing documents of the early church, implicitly affirms Foley's assumption when he notes in *The Apostolic Tradition* (Oxford Univ. Press, 1992) that "It is often . . . difficult to determine when the New Testament authors are citing topical prayer-forms with which they are familiar and when they are not, or even to separate hymns from prayers, since both may employ a similar construction" (p. 43, emphasis added). A familiar quotation usually attributed to St. Augustine, "Those who sing, pray twice," also seems to indicate a heritage of unified prayer and song.

Don Saliers once suggested that "at the heart of our vocation as church musicians and liturgical leaders is the question of how we enable the Church to 'pray well' — to sing and dance faithfully and with integrity" ("The Integrity of Sung Prayer,"

continued . . .

---

others to be evangelists, preachers, and teachers. But God also appointed some to be artists and musicians, dancers and poets. God's instructions for building the tabernacle were artistically elaborate. So, said the Lord to Moses, "I have called by name Bezalel . . . and I have filled him with divine spirit, with ability, intelligence, and knowledge in every kind of craft. . . . I have appointed with him Oholiab . . . and I have given skill to all the skillful, so that they may make all that I have commanded you" (Exod. 31:1-6).

We are God's image-bearers, endowed with a capacity to do as God does. Whereas God is a fabricator, we are prefabricators. To worship God we rely on stuff we have been given, sights we have seen, music we have heard. We, too, can create, but not "out of nothing," not like God. Still, using prefab materials, Christians are called

Worship 55, no. 4 [July 1981]: 293). Saliers's comment affords not only a renewal of the ancient unity between song and prayer but also a fresh way to plan music for worship.

By enabling our congregations to "pray well" we are changing the dialogue from one fixated on musical styles to one about the primary function of music within worship. Regardless of denominational perspective, liturgical heritage, or approach to worship, all Christians who gather pray. Prayer in its variety of functions may be the theme that binds into one body those assembled for worship. While prayer at the Lord's table may be primarily under the purview of the ordained clergy, most of the forms of prayer that permeate various approaches to worship belong to the people. Singing our prayers is a natural way for the people to claim their voice within worship. Rather than viewing the diversity of musical styles as divisive, perhaps we should regard them as many possible ways of praying. Part of teaching our congregations to pray well is to teach them to sing well and to sing deeply from the wells of Christian heritage and broadly from the diverse contemporary cultural possibilities that are signs of the Holy Spirit moving among us.

Such an approach may call for a fresh process of discernment when choosing music for worship. Some of the most common questions asked when selecting music are these: Are the people familiar with the music? Will the congregation respond positively to the music? Is the music thematically relevant? Is it uplifting? Is the text based in Scripture? These questions along with others are not to be dismissed. When the focus is on sung prayer, however, the function of music in worship becomes more precisely focused. Does this music pray well?

---

to bring the firstfruits of their minds and hands to God. Sculpted marble and rough-hewn wood may stand as a baptismal font. Raku pottery may grace the Lord's table. Liturgical dancers, ages seven to fifty-seven, may interpret a song of praise. A readers' theater troupe may dramatize the text for the day. Children may sign "Create in Me a Clean Heart" as the congregation sings this prayer of confession and renewal.

In these and so many other ways, worship is engagement. It is a holy meeting between God and God's people, involving a wide range of human emotion and physical expression — all the features of a complex conversation. Mysteriously, that conversation takes place both in this world and in the world to come, both in our time and beyond it. It takes place not only between God and God's people, but also among God's people. Given that God's people comprises

At what point in the worship experience does this sung prayer best fit – invocation, praise, adoration, petition, confession, blessing? Can the people participate fully in this prayer? Will this sung prayer help to unite those gathered into one body? Will the sung prayer aid the church as it prays for the needs of the world? These questions, added to those already asked, sharpen the focus of our music from performance and quibbling over musical styles to effective congregational singing and praying.

By focusing on sung prayer, we may even surprise ourselves, discovering that different musical structures, or forms, help us pray in different ways. In hymns, whose music is repeated with each stanza, the meaning of the text is communicated sequentially. By contrast, Praise and Worship or Contemporary Worship Music (CWM) formats are primarily cyclical. While these songs may seem repetitive or mantra-like, in many cases they are actually more similar to theme and variation in the hands of skillful musicians who know how to modulate the tempo, dynamics, and accompaniment to encourage variety. Varied repetition of this sort creates a musical space in which one may pray above and through what is being prayed through song. The music of Taizé, the Iona Community, and ethnic communities of faith often functions in this way as well. Refrain forms are a hybrid structure, combining some of the benefits of a sequential progression of ideas over several stanzas with the cyclic recurrence of the refrain.

Rather than "What shall we sing?" therefore, might we ask, "How shall we pray?"

---

believers of every land and era, we may expect the conversation to be as rich as anything human beings can do.

Worship Is *Narrative* Engagement

Ultimately this conversation is about a story. Indeed, it is about *the* story — the story of salvation, the effect of God's redeeming love. This is why we say worship is narrative engagement, not just contemplative engagement. In worship we certainly do contemplate the goodness of the Lord, but God's goodness is inseparable from God's role in the story. Nor is worship first of all evangelistic engagement. While some nonbelievers will always be among those who gather in any church on a Sunday morning, and while believers and nonbelievers alike will hear invitations to holy living and fellowship in Christ, worship is what the body of believers, called apart from the world, does before the throne of the Redeemer. Services primarily for seekers are a crucial part of the church's ministry, and shame on those lofty believers who scorn them; still, evangelism and worship are distinct activities with distinct goals. What this means for Christian worship is that, even with maximal sensitivity to the seekers among us, there will be some practices that seem strange to them, such as confessing sin, or eating and drinking the body of our Lord.

What might it mean to rehearse, or reenact, the narrative of redemption in worship?

If we think of the Christian story as one of creation, fall, and redemption, then the incarnation, death, and resurrection of Christ form the center of redemption, the epitome of God's saving grace.

> "We do not always think of repentance as worship . . . it can be much easier to sing a rousing hymn than to turn away from our favourite sin."
>
> Graham Kendrick, *Worship* (Eastbourne, England: Kingsway, 1984), p. 26

Meanwhile, God's covenant of grace binds a people to God — a people whose calling is to be a blessing to all. The end of the story will be the "new heaven and earth" in which God's perfect shalom will finally reign. What happens in worship is that we look at this narrative through different lenses. The scope of one lens is covenant renewal; the scope of another is the life of Christ; and the scope of another, the span of history, creation to re-creation. Each of these lenses has a field of vision that overlaps the others, and yet each field is also distinct. So it will help to consider each in turn.

Narrative Worship: Covenant Renewal

In Scripture, "covenant" is one of the chief means for administering the relationship between God and God's people. In the culture of the Ancient Near East, a covenant was a royal agreement, made between a sovereign and that sovereign's peers or subjects. It defined and coordinated a relationship, and commitments on both sides were sealed with oaths and ceremonies. In a similar fashion, God, the Sovereign of sovereigns, made covenants with his people. They defined and coordinated a preexisting relationship: I will be your God, says the Lord to Abraham, and your descendants shall be my people. I will be your God, says the Lord to the Israelites, gathered at the foot of Sinai, and you shall be my people. I will be their God, says the Lord through the prophet Jeremiah about the houses of Israel and Judah, and they shall be my people.

Scripture's covenants extend to believers today. To be in Christ is to be in the covenant of grace, which, again, reminds us both *who* we are and *whose* we are:

> You are a chosen race, a royal priesthood, a holy nation, God's own
> people, in order that you may proclaim the mighty acts of him who
> called you out of darkness into his marvelous light. Once you were
> not a people, but now you are God's people; once you had not re-
> ceived mercy, but now you have received mercy. (1 Peter 2:9-10)

In the Old Testament, we read not only of covenants but also of their confirmation and renewal at significant points in Israel's history. So, in Exodus, the covenant with Abraham is renewed at Mount Sinai in chapter 19, explained for a number of chapters, and then confirmed in chapter 24. God's covenant is ceremonially read, the people make their vows ("Everything the Lord has spoken we will do"), and blood is shed. "This is the blood of the covenant," says Moses as he sprinkles it upon the people. Forty years later, the people of Israel gather on the plains of Moab, waiting to enter the Promised Land on the other side of the Jordan, but first the covenant must be recalled, its conditions restated, and the people's promises reiterated. By the end of the book of Joshua, the Israelites have waged

"Creative variations in worship grow out of the basic meaning and themes of worship. Worship is a stimulant, not a product, of creativity."

C. Welton Gaddy and Don W. Nixon, *Worship: A Symphony for the Senses*, vol. 1: *Resources* (Macon, Ga.: Smyth and Helwys, 1995, 1998), p. 3

Communion in Prayer

Philip W. Butin

In contrast to the corporate nature of worship, you might be accustomed to thinking of prayer as a more personal kind of communion with God. Prayer is certainly deeply personal. But for Christians whose God is the Trinity, *personal* is not the equivalent of *individual,* and it is certainly not the opposite of *corporate.* Our identity as persons is in our relatedness. Because we *are* the body of Christ, all prayer is corporate (the Latin *corpus* is the word for "body") and interpersonal, whether we pray alone, with a friend, or in a large congregation. We are members of one another.

In fact, prayer is one of God's most wonderful and mysterious ways of linking us together as Christians. This is the "communion of the saints," a phrase from the familiar Apostles' Creed of our baptism. It refers to all of God's people through-
out history and around the world. In prayer, God the Spirit connects and unites us with the whole body of God the Son throughout time and space, everyone whom God the Father has called. In this Trinitarian *koinonia* of prayer, the normal physical limitations that our createdness would ordinarily place on our ability to be in communion with one another are mysteriously transcended. As we pray, the Holy Spirit connects us interpersonally with other Christians of all times and places as members of Christ's one body. This is true whether they live in this world or in God's presence, and whether they are traveling, or going to school in another city, or suffering miles away in the hospital, or enduring persecution on the other side of the world. It is God's own interpersonal communion within the Trinity that is the basis, pattern, and dynamic of the communion we share with other believers through prayer.

Excerpt from *The Trinity* (Louisville: Geneva, 2001), p. 104.

---

a successful campaign against the Canaanites. God so helped them that the land is theirs. Now, again, the covenant must be renewed, its promises reiterated. Centuries pass. The Israelites are dragged into exile. But they return, and when Nehemiah's armed masons complete the reconstruction of Jerusalem's wall, once again the Israelites gather to read the Law, to recall the covenant, to confess their sins, and to renew their promises (Neh. 8–10).

Today, our worship is a little like these ancient Israelite ceremonies. In worship, the Word and the songs, confession and blessing, remind us *who* we are and *whose* we are. They remind us that we, too, are the people of God, called to proclaim God's mighty acts. We're covenant children, adopted by God in Christ, and our time of worship thickens the covenant bond. This is why sacraments and ordinances are such a significant part of Christian worship. These are the new memorials of God's covenant promises for today. Just as the circumcision of infant boys and the sharing of the Passover meal were signs of God's covenant promises to Israel, so baptism and the Lord's Supper are signs of God's covenant promises to us. Through them we remember and rehearse the events that have put us in our primary "social location," which is "in Christ." Baptism, for instance, tells us that we were buried with Christ in his death and raised with Christ in his resurrection, and that our baptism now identifies us with Christ in the ritual of dying and rising (Rom. 6:1-11; Col. 2:12). Or, in a related meaning, baptism shows us that just as water washes away filth, Christ's blood washes away sin (Titus 3:5).

The Lord's Supper is a covenant sign, too. When Moses sprinkled blood on the people of God at Sinai, he declared to them, "This is the blood of the covenant." When Jesus Christ served the bread and the cup to his disciples, he declared to them, "This is my body," and then, "This is my blood of the covenant, which is poured out for many" (Matt. 26:28; Mark 14:24). That's the gospel according to Matthew and Mark. According to Luke, "This cup that is poured out for you is the new covenant in my blood" (Luke 22:20). Christ's blood is the sign of the new covenant anticipated by the prophet Jeremiah (31:31-34), the covenant whose central figure towers over Moses and Abraham. The bread of life and the cup of salvation that we pass to one another in worship are covenant signs. Like the waters of baptism, they identify us as people of Christ's death and resurrection and of all that they mean.

Since worship is covenant renewal, sacraments and ordinances belong inside of it — not out on the church patio for a few family and friends; not in another room for those who think they might like to participate this time. The baptismal font and the Lord's table do not memorialize *my* faith. They memorialize the Christ of *our* faith, whose death and resurrection are the seal of the covenant, the promise of new life.

The Difference between Evangelism and Worship

Marva J. Dawn

The difference [between evangelism and worship] can be illustrated easily. When leading worship seminars, I usually hold up an 8″ × 10″ school picture of my husband, to whom I've been joyfully married for 110 months and 21 days (as I write this). I tell the audience all about Myron — what a wonderful elementary school teacher he is, how magnificently beautiful are the gardens he grows, how gently he cares for me in my plethora of physical handicaps — all this to introduce him to listeners, as in evangelism. But is that how I will talk to him when I arrive home after several days away teaching? No, then I will speak to him words of adoration and love, listen to what he tells me about his work (how he has intervened in the world), talk with him about my own work (how might I have been more faithful?), sort out problems with him, and so forth — as in worship. Our conversations will be in the language of mutual intimacy and growth for the purpose of strengthening our relationship, rather than in the idiom of introduction.

Worship is the language of love and growth between believers and God; evangelism is the language of introduction between those who believe and those who don't. To confuse the two and put on worship the burden of evangelism robs the people of God of their responsibility to care about the neighbor, defrauds the believers of transforming depth, and steals from God the profound praise of which he is worthy.

Of course, the distinction is not total, for if believers worship with gladness and passion, anyone not yet a part of the community certainly will be attracted to the One who is the object of their worship. But to focus the worship upon evangelistic introduction deprives believers of deeper nurturing toward Churchbeing and deprives God of the intimate and involved worship due him from the Church.

Excerpt from *A Royal "Waste" of Time: The Splendor of Worshiping God and Being Church for the World* (Grand Rapids: Eerdmans, 1999), p. 124.

Narrative Worship: Centered on Christ

Since Christ is the central figure of the new covenant, he is also the central focus of all authentic Christian worship. Christ is both the one whom we worship and the one through whom we worship, by the power of the Holy Spirit.

Christ is also the one whom we memorialize in our worship, or at least we memorialize the events of Christ's life, which secured our salvation. This is the gospel we proclaim, the message we bring to the nations. So with respect to worship, the question we ask ourselves is this: Do we enjoy a fullness of remembrance of Christ? Do we proclaim the fullness of the gospel as expressed throughout all of Scripture and in the entirety of Christ's life?

Different churches meet this calling in different ways. For one church, it may mean preaching through the Gospel of Luke, perhaps beginning in December and finishing in April. It may mean crafting a series on Old Testament prophecies, or Old Testament characters who prefigure the Messiah, showing how prophetic promise reaches its fulfillment in the incarnate Christ.

When the founders of Harvard wrote their university's statement of mission, they declared that the main end of life "is *to know God and Jesus Christ which is eternall life,* Jn. 17.3, and therefore to lay *Christ* in the bottome, as the only foundation of all sound knowledge and Learning."[14] Throughout the centuries Christians have sought to do the same with respect to worship, to "lay Christ in the bottome" of the church's devotional practices. Even before the church was split between East and West in the eleventh century, Christians developed a yearly rhythm for worship, a cycle of seasons and feast days that follow the life of Christ. That cycle is often known as the liturgical year, and its steady movement through the seasons of joy and sorrow and joy is enjoyed by millions of Christians throughout the world every year.

To some, the liturgical year seems foreign. It seems officious, threatening to become more important than the life of Christ itself. True enough. As with any Christian practice, for some the liturgical year can become a sentimental ritual or thoughtless habit. But, according to its ancient intent, revived and thriving in churches throughout the world today, the liturgical year can also be an enriching devotional pattern, a narrative ostinato that orders the recurring motifs of our faith.

The year begins with the season of Advent, a time when Chris-

14. "New Englands First Fruits," quoted in Perry Miller and Thomas H. Johnsons, *The Puritans* (New York: American Book Company, 1938), p. 702.

ST. PATRICK'S BREASTPLATE

Patrick of Ireland (389-461)

I bind unto myself the name,

the strong name of the Trinity,

by invocation of the same,

the Three in One, the One in Three,

of whom all nature has creation,

eternal Father, Spirit, Word.

Praise to the Lord of my salvation,

salvation is of Christ the Lord. Amen.

Our Baptismal Calling

Philip W. Butin

Christian belief in the Trinity is ultimately about God's identity. Who is this God whom we know, worship, and serve? Why this God and not some other? The answer to that question is this: Our God is Yahweh: the One whose identity is definitively personal because it is established, revealed, and declared in divine words, commitments, and acts. Our God is Yahweh, the One who has taken and continues to take shape in human history, we can go on to say: Our God is Yahweh, the One who raised Jesus Christ from the dead in the power of the Holy Spirit, into whose triune name we are baptized. Our God is the Father, Son, and Holy Spirit, who created us to participate in God's own Trinitarian *koinonia,* and to live joyfully in that

---

tians draw alongside the Hebrews of the Old Testament. Inspired by the ancient prophets, we share the longing of the people of God for the anointed one, the Messiah. But Advent is not only a season of hope, it's also a season of sorrow. Again, along with the prophets, we repent of our sins and lament the evil that enshrouds us in darkness, for this is why our Messiah must come.

Just as darkness scatters when the Light shines, so Advent ends when Christmas arrives. On Christmas Day we celebrate the incarnation of Christ, the "humanization" of the second person of the Trinity. Christ came as a human to do for us what no one of us could do for ourselves, much less for another. Jesus Christ entered the world to offer the penance we owe. By the whole course of his life, and then by his death, he stood under the misery of the world's sin, absorbed evil without passing it on, and therefore cut the terrible lines

koinonia with one another in the church. Our God is the Father, Son, and Holy Spirit, whose gracious mission to the world overflows from the *koinonia* of God's own generous mutual self-giving.

If Trinitarian faith is about God's identity, then our shared baptism in the strong name of the Trinity is ultimately about *our* identity as God's people. That identity, that confidence of *who we are,* grows out of our conviction and experience of *Whose we are.* We are baptized. Our triune God holds us firmly and securely in the divine embrace. We are baptized. Our identity is constituted by our relationships with God and one another in the baptismal community, the church. We are baptized. In life and in death, we belong — not to ourselves — but to the God who proved faithfulness in raising Jesus from the dead by the power of the Spirit.

Our baptism in the strong name of the Trinity is our confidence of our God, our identity, and our belonging. Our baptism is also our calling. Baptism calls us to embrace and participate in the triune God's own mission to the world. . . .

The strong name of the Trinity was first written in remembrance of Jesus' personal missionary call to his followers. There are no clearer words with which to articulate our baptismal calling.

All authority in heaven and on earth has been given to me. Go therefore and make disciples of all nations, baptizing them in the name of the Father and of the Son and of the Holy Spirit, and teaching them to obey everything that I have commanded you. And remember, I am with you always, to the end of the age. (Matt. 28:18-20)

Excerpt from *The Trinity* (Louisville: Geneva Press, 2001), pp. 117-18.

---

of lawlessness and revenge that have looped down the centuries from the time of Cain and Lamech (Gen. 4).

In churches today, we often scrunch up history, rushing the wisemen to the manger on Christmas Day to stand alongside the shepherds. But the church has always remembered that these two visitations, the first by local Jews and the second by Gentiles who had "traveled afar," have different meanings, and so they are observed on different days. The shepherds stay with Christmas but the Magi get Epiphany, which means "manifestation." On Epiphany, Christians remember that Jesus Christ is the manifestation of God's salvation for every tribe and race and language and people.

In similar fashion, the liturgical year follows the rest of Christ's life, celebrating the significance of each stage for our salvation. After Epiphany comes a time to remember Christ's ministry, the baptism that began it and then the transfiguration that confirmed it. Then for forty days the church observes Lent, a season of repentance and renewal, of remembering that Christ took up his cross and calls his disciples to take up theirs (Matt. 16:24; Mark 8:34; Luke 9:23). Lent culminates in Holy Week, the memorial days of Christ's Passion: the triumphal entry on Palm Sunday, the Last Supper on Maundy Thursday,[15] and the crucifixion on Good Friday. Easter marks Christ's resurrection, the climax of the liturgical year and of all history until its end. More than just a holiday, Easter is a holy season of fifty days. Forty days in, the church marks Christ's ascension into heaven, his royal accession to the right hand of God; and at the fiftieth day, Christians celebrate Pentecost, the outpouring of the Holy Spirit, the agent of Christ's action in and through the church today.

> "It might be that the liturgical year is so powerful (and so scandalous) exactly because it reflects the central motif of God's own self-revelation. . . . The liturgical year is inescapably incarnational."
>
> Mark W. Oldenburg, "Liturgical Year: Within the World, Within Its Time," in *Inside Out: Worship in an Age of Mission*, ed. Thomas H. Schattauer (Minneapolis: Fortress, 1999), p. 105

The season that follows is a long one, and is often referred to with the unassuming title "Ordinary Time." Many churches begin this season with Trinity Sunday and end it with Christ the King Sunday, the last Sunday before the first Sunday of Advent.

Again, such a pattern for worship might seem merely ceremonial. But just as the seasons of summer, fall, winter, and spring, and all the traditional gatherings of friends or family that punctuate each one — just as these seasons and events repeat themselves, but with variations as our lives change, so it is with the liturgical year. It's the reprise of deep words and music that means something more, something new, to Christians after another year of following Christ through joy and sorrow and joy again.

Rehearsing the life of Christ and the way of salvation gives Chris-

---

15. According to the American Heritage Dictionary, "Maundy" comes from the Middle English "maunde," which comes from the Old French "mande," a derivative from the Latin phrase *novum mandatum*, or "new commandment." This phrase refers to Jesus' words to the apostles in the upper room, "I give you a new commandment . . ." (John 13:34).

tians "power to comprehend, with all the saints, what is the breadth and length and height and depth" of the love of Christ (Eph. 3:18).

Narrative Worship: Creation to Re-creation

We may see worship as covenant renewal, and we may see it as a way to follow the life of Christ. But both of these narrative visions fit inside a larger one — the all-encompassing narrative of creation, fall, redemption, and consummation. Two chapters ago, in our discussion of culture, we explored these stages of the biblical drama and their significance for our understanding of both our place in the world and the world's place in us. It will now be enough to mention only a few ways in which this biggest narrative affects Christian worship.

First, because God's good creation has been only corrupted, not destroyed, we find much of it still fresh and good, and may say so in worship. Because God renews creation, the "earth and all stars sing to the Lord a new song," and we may join them. Following the patterns of the ancient Hebrew poets, we may use contemporary psalms, perhaps read or sung responsively, to praise the Creator. In celebrating sacraments, ordinances given and received with the earthy elements of bread, wine, and water, we thank God for old gifts with new meanings. Sacraments use the good things of creation to mediate the new creation. In preaching the gospel, we may widen the frame from sin and grace to *nature,* sin, and grace. We can't preach grace without the knowledge of sin, but we can't preach sin without the knowledge of the greatness that sin has spoiled. Human beings (Saint Augustine called us "a little piece of God's creation") have been crowned with God's own steadfast love and mercy. These confer on humans a kind of dignity. If we see a drunken man mumbling and lurching along a public sidewalk, and then pausing to urinate on it, we are not watching an animal that has forgotten its potty training. We are watching the degradation of a king. (Sermons on sin need a tragic feel to them that fits the fall of royalty.)

Creation is the platform and presupposition of the whole biblical drama, and therefore of worship. Because we are image-bearers of God, redeemed in Christ, some of the original goodness persists in renewed form. Among especially our artists, writers, dancers, and musicians, such goodness yields art that reflects goodness right back to God. Indeed, churches may well commission such works to enhance their acts of worship, just as God did for his dwelling place among the Israelites.

> "There is nothing morbid about the confession of sins, so long as we go on to give thanks for the forgiveness of sins. It is fine to look inwards, so long as it leads us immediately to look outwards and upwards again."
>
> John Stott, *Christian Basics* (Grand Rapids: Eerdmans, 1969), p. 122

Still another implication of respect for creation in worship is one we've already noted: God gave us bodies, with ears to hear, and eyes to see, and a voice to sing, and hands to gesture. All our senses and features may be employed in worship, the better to taste and see the goodness of the Lord, and the better to praise the Lord for it.

The fallenness of creation finds expression in our acts of confession and lamentation. Throughout the year, the psalms — not just cropped verses and pasted-together passages, but whole psalms — may give us a voice for both. According to Denise Ackermann, lament is the language suffering people use when they recover their voice. Psalms are the language we use when we need a voice other than our own.[16] Taking the psalms as a whole shows us that praise and lament complement one another in worship.

To make confession of sin a part of worship is simply good spiritual hygiene. We are taking out the garbage. We are also trying to work against our almost fathomless capacity for self-deception. Confession isn't a perfect antidote to self-deception because our shifty psyche, on its knees to confess sin, will generate only a short list. Still, to say with the people of God, "I am a sinner, saved by grace," is to die and rise with Jesus Christ.

16. Denise Ackermann, "A Voice Was Heard in Ramah: Lament and Healing in South Africa," Princeton, N.J., 14 April 2000, unpublished.

What follows is that preaching about sin needs to be done faithfully — that is, inside the cradle of grace. We do not preach about sin in a vacuum, or as if sin is of independent interest — let alone as if it is entertaining, the way it is on TV. We do not preach on sin as mere judgment or condemnation. In other words, Christians do not preach on sin as those who have no hope. The center of our religion is not our sin but our Savior. In fact, one reason Christians go to church is to declare there that creation is stronger than sin, and grace is stronger still.

Human redemption through Christ is signified by the very fact that we gather on the day of resurrection. God calls believers apart from the world for a time, to refresh our relationship to God in community with others, and to prepare the community for service. As we've seen, one refreshment is to sing "psalms, hymns, and spiritual songs" that praise God. Delighting in God puts believers right side up. Doing it in community lets us delight in each other's joy as well as in our own. The same goes for the presentation of offerings. People who have been blessed enough to have something to give are twice blessed by joining forces with others, some of whom are heroes in the area of giving. Together, we buoy up causes none of us can support alone.

In a healthy Christian service of worship, God's Word will be read and preached quite deeply into people's lives, and people will receive it as food that whets the same appetite it satisfies. The center of Christian preaching is God's grace in Jesus Christ, not our

On Calvary, on Calvary,
They crucified my Jesus.
They nailed him to the cruel tree,
And the hammer!
The hammer!
The hammer!
Rang through Jerusalem's streets.
The hammer!
The hammer!
The hammer!
Rang through Jerusalem's streets.

Jesus, my lamb-like Jesus,
Shivering as the nails go through his hands;
Jesus, my lamb-like Jesus,
Shivering as the nails go through his feet.
Jesus, my darling Jesus,
Groaning as the Roman spear plunged
* in his side;*
Jesus, my darling Jesus,
Groaning as the blood came spurting from
* his wound.*
Oh, look how they done my Jesus.

James Weldon Johnson, "The Crucifixion," in *God's Trombones* (New York: Penguin, 1927)

Mystery of Mysteries!

Justo L. González

Although the church gathers in a multitude of places, and in each of those places only some of its members are present, it is never just a piece or a part of the church that worships. Worship is a communal act of the whole church. Either the entire church worships, or the act is not the worship of the church at all. I say that this is a reflection of the Trinity because when a Person of the Trinity acts, it is the entire Godhead that acts, and not just that particular Person.

Our worship is grand, not because we have a hundred-member choir, a powerful synthesizer, or a unique organ, but because with us also worship "angels and archangels, and all the company of heaven." And — mystery of mysteries! — it is grand because, no matter whether we will it or not, we too are part of those other worship services that we may find aesthetically displeasing or emotionally unsatisfying. We may be tempted to exclude them from our horizon of proper worship. They may seek to exclude us from their horizon of proper worship. But we are all included in the one worship with the company of heaven, as with angels and archangels, with all tribes and nations and languages and peoples, with organs and drums, with harpsichords and synthesizers, our praise rises to the throne, as incense to the sky.

---

efforts to look presentable. In Jesus' parable the prodigal son "came to himself." He "came to," which makes it sound as if his problem had been unconsciousness. Maybe that was part of it. He snapped out of whatever delusion took him out to the land of Nod. But the waiting father in the parable wants a feast — in fact a neighborhood blowout[17] — for a more serious reason: "My son was *dead* and is alive again!" The old, old story in Christian preaching and sacraments can't be expected to produce a catch of the breath in each retelling, as it does for ham-acting stump preachers. But cultivating the sense of passage from death to life is simply "getting the rhythm" of worship in union with Christ.

Songs, messages, and sacraments remind us of God's mighty acts in Jesus Christ, but they also refresh us for the way ahead. Offerings, too, express our faith not only in what God has done, but also in what God will keep doing. Part of the deal in the covenant of grace is that

---

17. Robert Farrar Capon, *The Parables of Grace* (Grand Rapids: Eerdmans, 1988), p. 144.

believers are redeemed not to feel better about themselves but to join God's redeeming effort in the world. They are saved to serve. Jesus taught disciples to pray for this: "Your kingdom come." He also sent disciples out into ministries of healing and teaching. Christian worship will have some of this same drive outward from worship to service.

In prayer, message, "minute for missions," and even bulletin announcements, a full-gospel church (charismatic or not) will do more at worship than answer the summons, "Let's just praise the Lord." At worship we do have time to adore God; we also have time to figure out ways of adoring God by living lives that bless people and the rest of creation, and thus signal the presence of the kingdom.

We may put matters here quite simply: A Christian church at worship is gathering strength to obey God's gracious directions for covenant life. As we saw back in chapter one, these include not only the famous ten commandments of the Old Testament but also a range of glad instructions for people who would follow Jesus. "Let your light shine. . . ." "Hate what is evil; hold fast to what is good." "Whatever is true, whatever is honorable . . . ; if there is any excellence . . . think about these things." "Pursue righteousness. . . ." "Remind them to be gentle." "Bear with one another." "Clothe yourselves with love." "Be imitators of God." "Strive first for the kingdom." "Bear one another's burdens and so fulfill the law of Christ."

These are all high callings, and no Christian can reach them all. We are all still under construction. Or, to use a main biblical image, we are still on the way to the city of God. We're pilgrims. To worship as a pilgrim is to let Psalms 42 and 63 and 137 bring their homesickness into our gatherings. In a fallen world, Christians are never entirely at ease. They're always feeling a little displaced.

In his book *¡Alabadle!* (a Spanish imperative to praise), Justo González shows how this dimension of every believer's life is poignantly felt among many Hispanics in the United States, and how it flavors their worship. The feeling, says González, is one of "belonging, yet not belonging." Mexican-Americans, to take the biggest example, can feel acutely that they are neither fully Mexican nor fully

American, and that they live "at the hyphen" between them.[18] Their sense is of being exiles who may not want to return to their country of origin, and who, in any case, cannot fully return to it. Their land has changed and so have they. At the same time, their new country views them as foreigners, even to some degree in church and even when everybody there is trying hard *not* to see them in this way.

According to González, the members of Anglo churches seem "installed" in their cultural setting, while Hispanics feel like exiles. And where does this difference manifest itself most acutely? It shows up in prayers for "the city that is to come."

> When in a Latino church we say "Thy Kingdom come" we say it with deep and almost desperate longing. When it is said in some of the churches of the dominant culture, one can almost hear a whispering undertone: "but not just yet."[19]

People whose earthly kingdoms have had a good year don't necessarily yearn for the kingdom of God to break in. They like their own setup just fine. And yet, authentic Christian worship, even if it has to import "desperate longing" from people at the hyphen, will point toward "a new heaven and earth." The Lord's Supper is a preview of the heavenly feast. Baptism puts God's sign of protection, like the mark on Cain, on people who will meanwhile be "fugitives and wanderers in the earth." Messages of the kingdom will imagine what it would be like for God's righteousness to fill the earth, and for justice and peace to embrace. In healthy Christian worship, says González, our singing is rehearsal "for the day when we shall 'laud and magnify' God's glorious name 'with angels and archangels, and with all the company of heaven.'"[20]

Wonderfully, the liturgical year crisscrosses the grand narrative

18. Justo L. González, introduction to *¡Alabadle!: Hispanic Christian Worship* (Nashville: Abingdon, 1996), p. 16.
19. González, *¡Alabadle!*, p. 18.
20. González, *¡Alabadle!*, p. 19.

of creation, fall, redemption, and consummation, allowing us multiple visions at the intersections. For example, as we noted earlier, in Advent the longing of the ancient prophets becomes our own. They longed for the Messiah to come; we long for the Messiah to come again. They lamented injustice in the land; we do too, even if we live in relative comfort. Once more, a ground-level demonstration that Christians in a dominant culture are Christians first, and members of their culture second, is the degree to which their longing for the city of God picks up intensity from their knowledge of the lives of people who live at the hyphen.

So, "Joy to the world! . . . No more let sin and sorrow rule, nor thorns infest the ground"; Christ has come, and "he makes his blessing known far as the curse is found." Christ has come, both to redeem and to restore, and although these missions have begun, neither will be finished till the last trumpet has been blown out straight.

In the interim, perhaps we have all been slicing our worship a little thin. This is true no matter what style of worship we prefer. Preferences, in fact, easily contract into parochial interests. But the worship of God, in union with Christ and the saints, easily expands us into persons fit for the worldwide kingdom of God. Praise, lament, grief; Advent, Christmas, Lent; creation, fall, redemption, consummation — these narratives frame Christian worship in ways big enough to stretch us all beyond our preferences.

Still, no matter how expansive our vision, worship always comes back to focus on one person, on one name that is above every name. For where two or three are gathered in my name, says the Lord, I am there among them. And so are all who are in him.

Juan Tamayo. *¡Presente!*

Maria Ibañez. *¡Presente!*

Jesucristo. ¡Presente!

Members of the Lilly Team

PHILIP W. BUTIN and DEBI EISENHOUR participated in this project as a minister-musician team from Shepherd of the Valley Presbyterian Church (USA), Albuquerque, New Mexico. While Eisenhour is still Director of Music Ministry there, Butin, since the time of our meetings, has been appointed president of San Francisco Theological Seminary, San Anselmo, California. He is author of *The Trinity* in the series Foundations of Christian Faith (Geneva Press, 2000).

MELVA WILSON COSTEN is the Helmar Emil Nielsen Professor of Worship and Music at the Interdenominational Theological Center in Atlanta, and is author of *African American Christian Worship* (Abingdon, 1993).

MARVA J. DAWN is a freelance theologian, author, and musician; Teaching Fellow in Spiritual Theology at Regent College, Vancouver, British Columbia; and author of many books including *Reaching Out without Dumbing Down: A Theology of Worship for This Urgent Time* (Eerdmans, 1995), *A Royal "Waste" of Time: The Splendor of Worshiping God and Being Church for the World* (Eerdmans, 1999), and *How Shall We Worship?* (Tyndale, 2003).

JOHN FERGUSON, nationally respected composer/arranger of music for congregation, choir, and organ, is the Elliot and Klara Stockdal Johnson Professor of Organ and Church Music as well as Cantor to the Student Congregation at St. Olaf College, Northfield, Minnesota.

TED A. GIBBONEY is an affiliate professor of church music and the Director of Chapel Music and Arts Programming at Christian Theological Seminary, Indianapolis.

JUSTO L. GONZÁLEZ is a historian and an advocate of Latino theological education. He was the founding President of the Association for Hispanic Theological Education, and the first director of the Hispanic Theological Initiative. He is the editor of ¡Alabadle!: Hispanic Christian Worship (Abingdon, 1996) and author of For the Healing of the Nations (Maryknoll, 1999).

MICHAEL S. HAMILTON is associate professor of history at Seattle Pacific University. His research interests range across religion and culture, fundamentalism and evangelicalism, and church music in America.

C. MICHAEL HAWN is a professor in church music and worship at Perkins School of Theology (Southern Methodist University), Dallas, Texas. He is the author of For the Living of These Days: Resources for Enriching Worship (Smyth and Helwys, 1995), Gather into One: Praying and Singing Globally (Eerdmans, 2003), and One Bread, One Body: Exploring Cultural Diversity in Worship (The Alban Institute, 2003).

CINDY K. HOLTROP is the director of the Congregational Ministries and Worship Renewal Grants program for the Calvin Institute of Christian Worship, Calvin College, Grand Rapids, Michigan. She is ordained in the Christian Reformed Church.

MARGO G. HOUTS is an ordained Presbyterian minister (PCUSA) currently serving a congregation in San Mateo, California. For over ten years she has taught a range of theology courses at Fuller Theological Seminary, San Francisco Theological Seminary, and Calvin College.

DUANE K. KELDERMAN was pastor of Neland Avenue Christian Reformed Church, Grand Rapids, Michigan, when our team first gathered. He is now Vice President for Administration at Calvin Theological Seminary. He is the primary author of *Authentic Worship in a Changing Culture* (CRC Publications, 1997).

CORNELIUS PLANTINGA JR. is ordained in the Christian Reformed Church. He was Dean of the Chapel at Calvin College and is now president of Calvin Theological Seminary, Grand Rapids, Michigan. He is author of *Beyond Doubt: Faith-Building Devotions on Questions Christians Ask* (Eerdmans, 2001) and *Engaging God's World: A Christian Vision of Faith, Learning, and Living* (Eerdmans, 2002).

ROBB REDMAN is pastor of Forest Hills Presbyterian Church, San Antonio, Texas. In the past he has served as a consulting editor to *Worship Leader* magazine, a vice president at Maranatha! Music, and director of the D.Min. program at Fuller Theological Seminary. His most recent book is *The Great Worship Awakening: Singing a New Song in the Postmodern Church* (John Wiley and Sons, 2002).

SUE A. ROZEBOOM was previously the associate for research and writing in the office of the Dean of the Chapel at Calvin College and is currently a doctoral student in the Liturgical Studies program at the University of Notre Dame.

LESTER RUTH is associate professor of worship and liturgy at Asbury Theological Seminary, Wilmore, Kentucky. He is the author of *A Little Heaven Below: Worship at Early Methodist Quarterly Meetings* (Abingdon, 2000) and *Accompanying the Journey: A Handbook for Sponsors* (Discipleship Resources, 1997). He is also the coauthor of *Creative Preaching on the Sacraments* (Discipleship Resources, 2002).

JOHN WILSON is editor of *Books & Culture,* editor at large of *Christianity Today,* and editor of "The Best Christian Writing" series.

JOHN D. WITVLIET is director of the Calvin Institute of Christian Worship and Dean of the Chapel of Calvin College. He teaches courses on worship, theology, and music at Calvin College and Calvin Theological Seminary, Grand Rapids, Michigan. He is editor of *A Child Shall Lead: A Sourcebook for Christian Educators, Musicians, and Clergy* (Choristers Guild, 2001), and author of *Worship Seeking Understanding: Windows into Christian Practice* (Baker Book House, 2003).